SURBITON 1

The History of SURBITON, HOOK, TOLWORTH *and* CHESSINGTON

In words and pictures

Tolworth Fountain, c. 1910, with Ewell Road stretching into the background. The corner building in the background is now a car-phone shop

SURBITON PAST

Richard Statham

Phillimore

1996

Published by
PHILLIMORE & CO. LTD.
Shopwyke Manor Barn, Chichester, West Sussex

ISBN 1 86077 026 6

Printed and bound in Great Britain by
BIDDLES LTD.
Guildford, Surrey

This book is dedicated
to my Parents
Jack and Barbara Statham

CONTENTS

List of Illustrations ix
Acknowledgements xi
A Note on the Sources xii
Preface xiii
Foreword xiv

1   A Patchwork of Manors 1
2   A Place of Battle 9
3   The Pleasure Resort 15
4   New Kingston 19
5   Coutts Take Control 29
6   New Responsibilities 37
7   Queen of The Suburbs 51
8   Fashion and Wealth 59
9   Edwardian Surbiton 73
10 A Prosperous Haven 89
11 Surbiton's War 105
12 Planning the Future 115

Index 127

LIST OF ILLUSTRATIONS

frontispiece: Tolworth Fountain, *c*.1910

Chapter 1

1. Late Bronze-Age spear and New Stone-Age flint 1
2. Pre-conquest mound enclosure ditch . . . 2
3. The summit of Castle Hill, Chessington 3
4. Barwell Court House 3
5. Engraving of Chessington church 4
6. Tithe barn from Tolworth 5
7. 1819 enclosure map of Tolworth 6
8. Detail from the northern section of the 1819 Tolworth enclosure map 6
9. Enclosure map of Chessington, 1825 7

Chapter 2

10. Colonel Henry Rich, Earl of Holland 11
11. Lord George and Lord Francis Villiers 12
12. Title page of 'The Decoy, Or A Practice of the Parliaments' 13

Chapter 3

13. Rocque map of Surrey, 1762 16
14. The Epsom Coach 17
15. *Waggon and Horses*, Surbiton Hill 17
16. Map of Surrey by A. Bryant, *c*.1822 . . . 18

Chapter 4

17. Surbiton Place 19
18. Kingston 'Inclosure Notice' 20
19. Engraving of the first Surbiton station, *c*.1850 21
20. Surbiton railway cutting with steam train, *c*.1930 21

21. Southborough House, *c*.1960 22
22. Rose or Regency Cottage 23
23. Hill House, Surbiton, 1898 24
24. Pooley's estate map of Surbiton 25

Chapter 5

25. Wanted poster 30
26. The first St Mark's Church 31
27. Engraving of St Mark's Church, *c*.1850 32
28. Albury House in 1931 33
29. The *Rising Sun Inn*, Clay Hill 34
30. *Bonesgate Inn*, Chessington, *c*.1900 36

Chapter 6

31. Chairmen of Surbiton Improvement Commissioners 37
32. Archdeacon Burney, Vicar of St Mark's 39
33. Christ Church, Surbiton, 1863 40
34. St Andrew's Church, *c*.1900 41
35. St Matthew's Church 42
36. Congregational Church, *c*.1888 43
37. Wesleyan Church, Ewell Road, *c*.1910 . 45
38. Regatta at Raven's Ait 46
39. Yachting at Surbiton 49
40. Mrs Sterry; five times Wimbledon Singles Champion 50

Chapter 7

41. Map of Surbiton, 1888 51
42. Interior of Oak Hill Lodge 52
43. Surbiton Cottage Hospital, 1883 54
44. Langley Avenue 55
45. Surbiton Station, *c*.1880 56
46. Half-Shilling Butchers, *c*.1854 58

Chapter 8

47. Surbiton Assembly Rooms,
    Maple Road, *c.*1900 60
48. Jane Dewhurst 62
49. Admiral Jellicoe 63
50. Monsieur George Pigache
    and family 64
51. Members of the Stickley family
    after a shoot, *c.*1900 65
52. John James Stickley's prize carthorses . . . 66
53. The top of Ewell Road, *c.*1900 66
54. Victoria Road, *c.*1890 68
55. Adelaide Road, Surbiton, *c.*1927 69
56. The Portsmouth road junction with the
    Uxbridge road, *c.*1927 69
57. Cornfield on the Ewell road, *c.*1900 . . . 70
58. St Mary's Church congregation 72

Chapter 9

59. Patients at the Gables 74
60. The Gables theatre 75
61. The Watercress and Flower
    Girls Mission 76
62. Patient Ass, or the Surbiton ratepayer . . 76
63. Adolf Zimmern 77
64. Tram passing the Surbiton Clock Tower
    and Claremont Road 78
65. London and Suburban
    Omnibus Co. Bus, 1906 79
66. Tramway terminus, *c.*1910 79
67. Opening of Tolworth Fountain 80
68. Surbiton Drying and Cleaning Works . . 81
69. W.B. Farmer, Ewell Road 81
70. J. Lane and Son, Brighton Terrace 82
71. W. A. Ratledge, Victoria Road 84
72. Dyson Coal and Coke Merchants 84
73. Claremont Road after a snowstorm 85
74. J.E. Allen, Draper and Milliner 85
75. Electric Parade, Brighton Road 86
76. Unveiling of war memorial 88

Chapter 10

77. Hook Bowls Club outing, *Southborough
    Arms*, *c.*1920 90
78. William Cowley 92
79. Hook Cricket Club, *c.*1920 93
80. Betty Nuthall 94
81. St Paul's School, Hook, 1922 95
82. Arthur Pointer's grocery shop, Hook
    Road 96
83. Berrylands advertisement, 1934 97
84. Gilders Road, Chessington 98
85. Warren Drive, Tolworth 99
86. Messrs. Thorogood's Haycroft Estate . 100
87. Interior of Surbiton station after
    rebuilding, 1938 101
88. Tolworth Broadway in the 1930s 102

Chapter 11

89. The Rev. Featherstone and Choir of
    St Paul's, Hook 106
90. St Mark's Church 108
91. Surbiton ARP districts 109
92. The British Restaurant, Hook 110
93. 'Salute the Soldier', 1944 111
94. VE celebrations at Gladstone Road . . 112

Chapter 12

95. The seal pool at Chessington Zoo . . . 116
96. Open-topped horse, *c.*1940 117
97. Andre Rubber Factory, 1958 118
98. Gala Factory, *c.*1958 118
99. The Tolworth Odeon before
    demolition in the 1950s 119
100. Kingston Road, Tolworth 119
101. Claremont Road 120
102. Tolworth Broadway 121
103. Victoria Road 122
104. Winthrop House and Surbiton
    station 123
105. Surbiton Lagoon, *c.*1960 124

ACKNOWLEDGEMENTS

THE majority of illustrations in this book have been taken from the Kingston Borough Archives and the photographic collection of Kingston Museum and Heritage Service held at the Local History Room, North Kingston Centre, Richmond Road, Kingston. Most of the other photographs come from the collection of the Surbiton and District Historical Society, to which the author owes a great debt of thanks for kindly making the photographs available, and for granting permission to reproduce the photographs in this book.

The author is particularly grateful for the help and support of Miss Sheila Brewster, Chairman, Mrs. Ann Glover, Honorary Secretary, Mr. Reginald Lockyer, Vera Dowling and in particular Mr. and Mrs. Peter Daniels of the Surbiton and District Historical Society for all their help and support. Thanks are also due to the Surrey Record Office for permission to reproduce two illustrations free of charge, Wimbledon Tennis Museum for granting permission to reproduce two photographs free of charge, to Ivan MacQuisten, Editor of the *Surrey Comet*, for granting permission to reproduce two items from the newspaper free of charge and to The Frith Collection, Shaftesbury, Dorset. Thanks also to the British Museum.

The author would like to thank colleagues at Kingston Museum and Heritage Service for their help and encouragement and also for proof reading. Particular thanks are due to Tim Everson, Local History Officer, Jill Lamb, Assistant Archivist and Paul Hill, Collections Manager. Especial thanks to Anne McCormack for all her support and encouragement and for giving me the opportunity to write this book.

The author also wishes to thank the staff of the Surrey Record Office for their assistance to the author in carrying out research; in particular to Dr. David Robinson, Maggie Vaughan-Lewis, Julian Pooley and Libby Lewis. Thanks also to Les Kirkin for photographs of original material. Thanks also to Dr. A.S. Bendall, Librarian, Merton College, Oxford.

As further reading on the subject of Surbiton, the author recommends *All Change* by June Sampson, published by News Origin Ltd. and *The Book of Kingston* by Shaan Butters, published by Baron Birch for Quotes Ltd. *Kingston upon Thames: A Pictorial History* by Anne McCormack, which is also published by Phillimore, includes further photographs from Kingston, Surbiton and Malden. The author also recommends *The Story of Hook in Kingston* by Marion Bone and *From Talworth Hamlet to Tolworth Tower* by Dorothy Ward.

Credits for particular photographs are as follows: Surbiton and District Historical Society, courtesy of Don Leeson, 17, 49; painting by Miss Waller, Surbiton and District Historical Society, 90; courtesy of P. Grevatt, Surbiton and District Historical Society, 16, 50; Surbiton and District Historical Society, courtesy of Mrs. Cowley, 78; Surbiton and District Historical Society, courtesy Mr. P. Daniels, 26, 39, 53; courtesy of Reginald Lockyer, 22; courtesy of *Surrey Comet*, 83, 93; courtesy of Wimbledon Lawn Tennis Museum, 40, 80; Surrey Record Office, print courtesy of Surbiton and District Historical Society, 44; copyright British Museum; 10, 11; Copyright Kingston Local History Room, reproduced courtesy of The Frith Collection, Shaftesbury, Dorset, 88, 95, 99-105; photograph by Richard Statham, 1, 3, 4; photographed from original material by Les Kirkin, Copyright Kingston Museum and Heritage Service, 7-9, 12, 13, 24, 31, 41, 59-61, 91, 92. All other photographs Copyright of Kingston Museum and Heritage Service.

A Note on the Sources

The main sources for *Surbiton Past* in order of importance are: the complete archive collection of the *Surrey Comet*, 1854—present day, held at the Local History Room, North Kingston Centre; *Thirty-Two Years of Self Government*, R. Richardson, 1888, Kingston Local History Room; the Kingston Borough and Oral Archives; the Public Record Office (including C14/280/25); the Pamphlet collection of the Kingston Local History Room; the British Library; the Surrey Record Office; the Victoria County History. A full list of primary sources is available on application to Kingston Museum, Wheatfield Way, Kingston KT1 2PS.

The author also acknowledges occasional use of secondary sources from the Kingston Local History Pamphlet Collection; and the following: 'The Story of Hook in Kingston' by Marion Bone; 'From Talworth Hamlet to Tolworth Tower', by Dorothy Ward; 'A Mansion Made from Matches', Doreen Ehrlich, *Surrey History*, Volume 4, no 4, 1992; Chessington Church Guides by Joan Garhard and Henry Harper; *The Book of Kingston* by Shaan Butters for information about oil mill and the railway; the following points in *All Change* by June Sampson: 'Disorderly scenes on Portsmouth Road', details about John Selfe, M. Pigache and Dr. Alfred Cooper; the reference number for the Thomas Pooley papers in the Public Record Office; £120,000 offered for Maple Farm Estate.

PREFACE

SURBITON'S image was dealt a blow in the 1970s when the television comedy series 'The Good Life' was first screened. To those who had never visited, Surbiton summoned up images of Margot Leadbetter and over-tended lawns. The reputation has persisted and in 1995 Liverpool City Council seriously considered adopting 'Liverpool—It's not Surbiton' as a marketing slogan to suggest the City's vitality and originality.

But Surbiton is not the faceless sprawl of popular myth. The place name does not derive artificially from 'suburb' as people wrongly assume, but dates back to Saxon times. The former Borough of Surbiton comprises neighbourhoods with distinct and rooted identities; the Improvement District of Surbiton with its Italianate villas and tree-lined streets: the ancient Manors of Tolworth and Chessington and the medieval hamlet of Hook. This book traces the history of each of these neighbourhoods, to prove the richness and depth of Surbiton Past.

FOREWORD

I AM pleased to introduce this new volume on Surbiton which is the result of painstaking original research undertaken by Richard Statham. The histories of Surbiton, Tolworth, Hook and Chessington have been brought together with fascinating photographs which will have wide appeal.

Surbiton Past provides illuminating insights into a rich, varied and often surprising story and is a welcome addition to our existing range of local books.

ANNE MCCORMACK

Heritage Officer,
Kingston Museum
and Heritage Service

A PATCHWORK OF MANORS

After the Thaw

SURBITON stands on London clay, overlain in places by gravel, brickearth and other types of clay. Until about 10,000 years ago, the district was in the grip of the Ice Age. At their greatest extent, glaciers reached as far as the northern Thames Valley. The Thames cut a deep channel during the colder phases, but in the warmer periods, gravel, silt and sand was deposited along the river.

At the end of the Ice Age, tundra was replaced by lush woodland and the Thames broke its banks, submerging stone axes and other human artefacts. Thames Picks, used for felling trees during the Middle Stone Age, have been discovered on submerged land at Raven's Ait. Flint tools, dated between about 8000 and 4000 B.C., have also been found at Alpine Avenue in Tolworth and Mansfield Road in Chessington. Many of these axes were specially shaped for cutting down trees and shaping wood.

Axes from the New Stone Age have been discovered in Tolworth and Chessington. These were often ground and polished and may have been used as trading exchanges or gifts—perhaps as part of wedding dowries. Finds from the Bronze Age include a spear head found in the river island of Raven's Ait; nearby Coombe Hill was an important bronze-working centre.

A small settlement existed in Alpine Avenue, Tolworth, during the Iron Age. The settlement was unusual because it was close to a larger enclosed settlement at nearby Old Malden. Items found at the site in 1991 include pottery fragments, fragments of loomweights, animal bone and fire-cracked burnt flints. Part of a gulley surrounding an Iron-Age hut was also found. Ditches and gulleys which suggest Iron-Age occupation have also been excavated at Mansfield Road, Chessington.

During the Roman period, the Surbiton district was skirted by Stane Street which ran from London to Ewell and from there to Dorking. The road ran close to a large villa on Ashtead Common, just over the present-day boundary of Chessington. Red tiles were made at this villa, which probably had authority over farms and homesteads in the surrounding area. Roman coins were also found near Barwell Court and, according to Brayley, near the Castle Hill in Chessington.

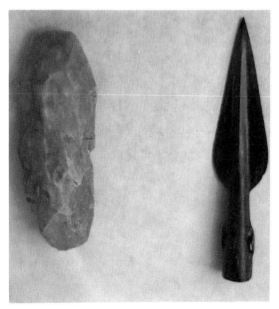

1 Right: late Bronze-Age spear head found in the river at Raven's Ait. The hooks on either side were used to bind the spear head to the handle. Left: adze of roughly cut flint dating from the New Stone Age and found in Chessington.

2 *Ditch of pre-conquest mound enclosure in the Grapsome, near Barwell Court, Chessington. It was destroyed by the Esher by-pass construction. Photographed in 1975.*

During the Saxon period, most of Surbiton was part of the Royal Estate of Kingston—the place name 'Cyingestun' means King's estate, palace or enclosure. The estate originally included Surbiton and Hook, but not Tolworth or Chessington. It also comprised Long Ditton, Kingston, Ham, Petersham, and part of present-day Malden.

At the Norman Conquest, the estate became a Royal Manor under the feudal system. Land holders were directly tenants of the King. Beyond the Royal Manor stretched a complex patchwork of manors held by other Lords. These were not united under local government with Surbiton until the late 19th and 20th centuries, when the histories of Tolworth, Chessington and Surbiton merged together.

Surbiton was part of Kingston Parish from Saxon times and lay within the Kingston Hundred—a wider administrative division which incorporated Richmond.

Surbelton, Surbeton, Surbiton

Several different origins have been suggested for the name Surbiton, which was not spelled in a standard form until the 19th century.

Surbiton and Norbiton seem to have derived their names from a common source. Biden, writing

in 1852, suggested that both names derived from the Anglo-Saxon 'bellen' which means, to shout or give alarm and 'ton', interpreted as meaning the site of a settlement. Thus the Bittoms would have been the site of the 'Belton' or chief watchtower, Norbiton would have been the north belltower and Surbiton or Surbelton would have been the site of the south belltower.

However, the name is more likely to be derived from the Saxon word 'bereton' which meant granary or grain store. Thus Surbiton was the south barton, or southerly farm on the estate.

Surbiton was mentioned in 1179, when John Hog, along with about twenty other freemen, granted land at Hook to Merton Priory on a 21-year lease at a payment of five shillings a year. The estate at Hook was initially called 'Grapellingeham'.

Surbiton was mentioned again in 1235, when the Prior of Merton granted to Kingston Parish the right to the produce of gardens, warrens and fields throughout the Manor and Parish of Kingston, including 'Surbeton'. A similar document from 1375 mentioned 'Sorbelton' as well as a dovecot at Barwell Court Farm at Hook.

As part of the Royal Manor of Kingston, Surbiton had to make a contribution to the feudal

3 *The summit of Castle Hill, Chessington, looking towards Copt Gilders. The hill was probably the site of a medieval moated homestead, possibly a hunting lodge to Chessington Park Manor. This stretched from Filby Road to Park Farm, Chessington.*

4 *The photograph shows the present Barwell Court House, with Georgian front. A farm on this site dates back to the Middle Ages. The farm adjoined the estate of Grapellingeham. In 1375, the emoluments of the vicar of Kingston included 'a dovecot at Berewell'. The Barwell Court Farm Estate later merged with the Grapellingeham Estate. This was leased by Merton Priory. The present house, auctioned in 1872, offered a 'nut walk' and fishpond, possibly of medieval origin.*

dues which Kingston owed to the king under charter. 'Surbeton' paid £1 2s. and 11½d. in 'quit rent' to the bailiffs and freemen of Kingston in 1413.

According to the *Victoria County History*, William Skerne, a descendant of Edward III though his mistress, Alice Perrers, won a licence to enclose a piece of land in 'Berowe' called the Fifteen Acres in 1439. This was the earliest recorded mention of 'Berowe' or Berrylands.

Hook

Hook was a part of the Royal Manor of Kingston before the Norman Conquest. Ditches discovered on Surbiton boundary during construction of the Esher by-pass are thought to have dated from before the Norman Conquest. They may have formed a fortified enclosure for Earl Tostig, who owned an estate stretching towards Claygate.

The name 'Hoke' was used by Merton Priory during a court case in 1223. By then, Hook was

5   South-west side of Chessington Church. Engraving, c.1800, with original spire. The south aisle was added in 1870.

6 The medieval tithe barn at Tolworth Court Farm, Kingston Road, Tolworth, 1967.

a small hamlet pushed against the heel of the Royal Manor, in an angle formed by the boundary of the Royal Manor—hence the descriptive name 'Hook'.

Tala's Worth

The origin of the name Tolworth, or Talworth, as it was often written, is obscure. The name may derive from Tala's Worth, meaning Tala's Enclosure; Tala, an unusual name, meant 'swift' or 'prompt' in Old English.

Unlike Hook, Tolworth was never part of the Royal Manor of Kingston or Kingston Parish. Instead it lay within the parish of Long Ditton. Tolworth was originally divided into three manors; Tolworth or Tolworth Court Manor, North Tolworth and South Tolworth. These had all been granted by King William to his loyal soldier, Richard de Tonbridge, lord of more than 170 other manors in England, including 35 in Essex, 95 in Suffolk, three in Cambridgeshire and two in Kent. The family name of Richard de Tonbridge was 'De Clare', derived from the name of one of the family manors in Suffolk.

Richard de Tonbridge, as overlord, granted the Manors of Tolworth to intermediary lords. He was also overlord to Chessington Manor.

Tolworth Manor

According to the Domesday Survey of 1086, Tolworth or Tolworth Court Manor was created from land owned by Alwin before the Norman Conquest, which had been granted to Richard de Tonbridge by King William. The land was in turn sublet by Richard to the Picot family. In 1291, Henry Picot granted eight acres of the manor to the Hospital of St John of Jerusalem.

By 1255 the land had passed to the de Planaz family. In that year, a dispute broke out between Ralph de Planaz and the prior of Merton over whether the prior should pay feudal service to Ralph for land which the priory held in Tolworth. Sixty-five years later, control of the manor had passed to Hugh Le Despenser, an ally of King Edward II who was then facing a rebellion raised by his Queen and her lover, Mortimer. In 1327 the manor passed to Edmund, Duke of Kent, after Hugh had been hung at Hereford on a 50ft. gallows. But Edmund was also sentenced to death in 1330 for opposing Mortimer's rule.

An audit of the Manor of Tolworth was taken in 1327. At this time, according to the *Victoria County History*, the manor estate included a moated mansion house with a gateway, drawbridge, two halls, six chambers, a kitchen and a bakery. The

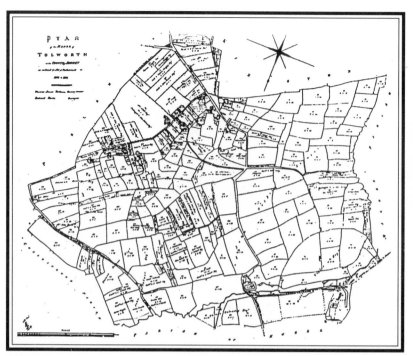

7 *1819 enclosure map of Tolworth showing the extent of Tolworth Court Manor. The fields to the north were originally part of Surbiton Common. Tolworth Lodge Farm is marked in the south beside the Hogsmill Stream. Further to the east lies Tolworth Hall. The Kingston by-pass now runs through the centre of the area marked on the map.*

8 *Detail from the northern section of the 1819 Tolworth enclosure map.*

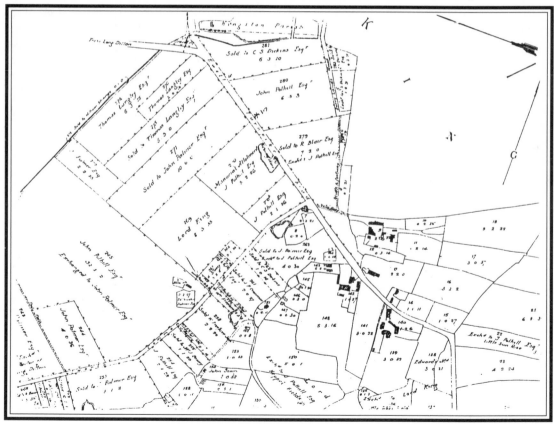

house also held a brewery and a chapel. Beyond the moat was a stable, two ox houses, a pig sty, a garden and a water mill, known as 'Brayest Mulne'. The Manor House stood at Tolworth Court Farm on Kingston Road between Tolworth and Ewell.

The manor later passed to Joan, 'Fair Maid of Kent', mother of King Richard II. Later owners included the distinguished Elizabethan courtier Sir Ambrose Cave and George Evelyn, grandfather of the diarist John Evelyn, who is credited with introducing gunpowder into England. In 1605 part of the manor was encroached upon when the boundaries of Nonsuch Park were extended.

Other Tolworth manors

North Tolworth was held before the Conquest by Edmer. After the Conquest, Richard de Tonbridge, granted lordship to his brother, Ralph. The manor remained under the control of the Clare family in 1314, but by 1349 it had fallen under the control of the Despensers. After 1440 North Tolworth Manor probably merged with the Manor of Long Ditton.

South Tolworth Manor also belonged originally to Richard de Tonbridge. The manor was later sublet to Merton Priory by Hugh of Isold. At the dissolution of the monasteries under Henry VIII, the land was annexed by Hampton Court Palace.

Chessington

The name Chessington has been spelt in many different ways, including Cisedune, Chissendon and Chyssyndone. The name probably derives from Cissa's Dene or hill, Cissa being the name of a Saxon owner. Originally part of Kingston Hundred, a county sub-division, Chessington later joined Copthorne Hundred.

After the Conquest, Richard de Tonbridge became overlord to Chessington Manor. This stretched from the boundary of Tolworth Manor along the present-day line of Cox's Lane towards Malden Rushett. It surrounded the Manor of Fream, which occupied a wedge of land around the present-day Chessington South Station.

Chessington Manor

Chessington Manor was created from the estate which had been held by a Saxon called Erding at

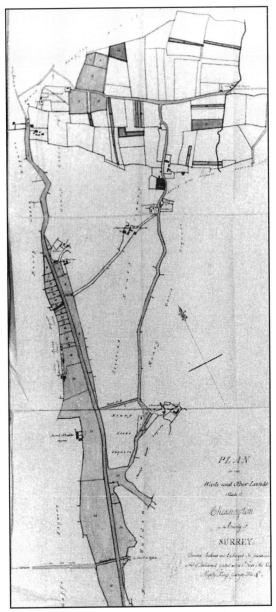

9 *Enclosure Map of Chessington, 1825. The original extent of Chessington Common is marked in dark grey to either side of the Leatherhead Road. Burnt Stub lies just west of the Chessington Common; Strawberry Hill House, today St Philip's School, is also marked. Garrison Lane and Moor Lane are both shown; the Old Harrow is just north of the Garrison Lane junction with the Leatherhead Road. Green Lane marks the eastern boundary of Fream Manor, held by the Penney Family. East of Green Lane was a strip of land belonging to Chessington at Hook Manor; further east lay the Merton College Estate.*

the time of King Edward the Confessor. After the Norman Conquest, the manor was sublet to Robert de Wateville, who also held land in Malden.

In 1249 part of Chessington Manor was bought by Walter de Merton, who also bought the Wateville Estate in Malden. In 1262, De Merton founded a 'House of Scholars' at Malden, supported with income from the estates at Chessington and Malden. The 'House of Scholars' was transferred to Oxford in 1264, where, with 20 students, it formed the nucleus of Merton College.

In 1279, by right of Charter already granted by Henry III, Merton College's holdings at Chessington were turned into a hunting park for the exclusive use of the master and scholars of Merton College; this was confirmed by Edward I in 1290. Chessington Park, as it came to be known, stretched between the present-day Filby Road and Park Farm; the Castle Hill mound may have been the site of the estate hunting lodge.

The rest of Chessington Manor, to the north and east, was held by Merton Priory. This estate became known as the Manor of Chessington at Hook and was held by Merton Priory until the dissolution of the monasteries.

Chessington Church was first mentioned in the records of Merton Priory dated 1174-1189. Richard, Bishop of Winchester, confirmed to the priory the right to derive income from 'the Chapel of Chissendon and the Church of Meldona'. At this time, Chessington was part of the parish of Old Malden. The chapel was transferred to the protection of Merton College, Oxford when the college acquired Chessington Park.

Fream Manor

The estate later known as Fream Manor was held by Magnus Swarthy before the Norman Conquest. After 1066, ownership of the estate was disputed between Miles Crispin and his father-in-law, Wigod of Wallingford. By 1279 it had fallen into the possession of Edmund, Earl of Cornwall.

The Manor House, later known as Chessington Hall, dated from around 1120 and survived on its original site on Garrison Lane until after the Second World War. 'Garrison' means grassy enclosure, suggesting that the manor was well provided with good farmland.

During the 13th century, the manor fell into the hands of Boxley Abbey in Kent. The abbey was famous for its 'Rood of Grace', a crucifix said to have the power of movement, which attracted many pilgrims. Some land in Chessington was held by Boxley Abbey in 1189 and in 1291. In 1291, the abbey was taxed £1 4s. for its Chessington holdings. In 1329, the abbot was pardoned for acquiring a personal rent in Chessington of 13s. 2d. from Clement le Taillour and Nicholas, son of Osbert atte Woodhall.

CHAPTER
2

A PLACE OF BATTLE

THROUGH the Tudor period, Surbiton remained part of the Royal Manor of Kingston. The Charter of Elizabeth I, granted in 1561, mentioned 'one tenement in Surpleton, with one barn and one pightell, containing one acre of land, by estimation 80 acres'. Rents from the estate were used to fund Kingston Grammar School in the Lovekyn Chapel. Surbiton was mentioned again in the King James I Charter of 1603 which gave Kingston the right to appoint JPs with authority over 'Surbeton'. The King Charles I Charter of 1638 confirmed this authority.

The Rocque map from 1762, the earliest complete map of the Surbiton district, gives a clear picture of what Surbiton was like before the transformations of the 19th century. Farmland was interrupted by wild commons of furze and bracket. Kingston Common opened up from the top of Surbiton Hill, widening along Ewell Road and stretching towards Hook and Tolworth. There was more common land along the road in Chessington and at Malden Rushett.

The Surbiton fishponds at the foot of the hill on Ewell Road are recorded on the Rocque map, but documents reveal that they dated from late medieval times. Thomas Hoke of Epsom bequeathed '1 shilling for the repairing of a pond betwixt Chesynton and Kyngston' in a will dated 9 October 1489.

Some of the ponds belonged to the Kingston Bailiffs. Camberley Pond, close to a piece of ground called the Slades, was leased by Bailiffs Thomas Agar and Henry Male in 1695 to Leonard Hammond for 5s. a year. Hammond then sublet the pond to William Talman, who had already leased adjoining land from the bailiffs. The leaseholder had the right to plant trees on Surbiton Common.

The Rocque map marks many roads and lanes crossing the commons and running between fields. From 1555, these were looked after by the parish, which sometimes struggled to maintain them properly. A Parliamentary survey of church lands made between 1649 and 1658 described the roads between Chessington and Malden as 'extreame foule and not passable in the winter season'. But some roads received funds for their upkeep from wills and bequests; in 1511, Cecily Hussie bequeathed 13s. 4d. 'to the hyway of Surbynton called Lamvale Almns'.

The Rocque map shows Burnt Stub, possibly built in 1348, which may have been used as an archery school in the reign of Queen Elizabeth. The name 'Burnt Stub' probably derives from the former practice of burning the stubs of trees in the surrounding woods and fields; there is no evidence that Oliver Cromwell or the Parliamentary armies ever burnt the house.

Land in Chessington was bought by Theophilus Colcock from Prudence Kerdall in 1666. Colcock, a Parliamentary supporter, was Kingston Bailiff during much of the period after the end of the Civil War. At the restoration of the monarchy, Colcock was expelled from the Kingston Court of Assembly because he had allegedly promoted some members of the Corporation and dismissed others in contravention of traditional procedure. He later lived in London, but maintained sufficient prosperity as a linen-draper to buy the Chessington land, which he later sold in 1674.

The only church in the district remained St Mary's at Chessington. At the Reformation, the bells, chalices and vestments of the church were sold to William Warde of Kingston for 7s. In 1568, the church acquired a precious communion cup, three and three quarter inches high, engraved with foliage round the bowl. Parish registers were maintained from 1656, although the church remained tied to the parish of Old Malden.

Royal Involvement

Local land ownership went through several enforced changes during the Tudor period.

Boxley Abbey and Merton Priory were both made to give up their lands in Chessington following the dissolution of the monasteries. Boxley Abbey was taken over by the Crown and the famous moving crucifix—the Rood of Grace—was apparently exposed as a mechanical fraud. The Boxley Estates of Fream were purchased by John Rychbell in 1547.

At the Dissolution, Merton Priory held land at Kingston, Tolworth, Chessington and Hook amounting to £1 16s. 1½d. These holdings were first annexed 'to the honour of Hampton Court' and later sold. Those parts of Chessington Manor held by Merton Priory were granted in 1557 to William Rigges and Peter Gearing. In 1610 the estate was bought by William Haynes, who had gained control of Fream Manor in 1594. The two estates remained united until 1742, when Thomas Hatton sold Chessington Manor but retained ownership of Fream. Merton Priory's former holdings at Hook, including Barwell Farm, were bought by Thomas Vincent in 1587. This land was later absorbed into the Lovelace Estate.

Merton College retained ownership of Chessington Park until Elizabeth I decided to develop Nonsuch Palace in Ewell. The site of the new palace belonged to the Earl of Arundel and the Queen looked for nearby land which she could exchange for the Nonsuch Estate.

In 1578 the Queen confiscated Chessington Park from Merton College so that she could offer the estate to Lord Arundel. The college were forced to grant to the Crown a 5,000-year lease on Chessington Park. This lease was then handed to Earl Arundel, who in turn relinquished the Nonsuch Estate. Shortly afterwards, Arundel sold on the lease to Lord Lumley, who then transferred it to the Goode family.

Merton College began legal proceedings in 1621 to recover the manor from the Goode family. In 1623 a pamphlet was produced by the college which claimed that the lease held by the Goode family was invalid, and that the assent of the college to the lease had been won by 'threats of violence'. Eventually a compromise was reached, and Merton College regained ownership of the estate in 1707.

Lord Villier's Last Stand

Surbiton was the scene in 1648 of one of the last episodes of the Civil War.

As the War reached its conclusion, supporters of the Royalist cause planned to raise a rebellion in Surrey. They hoped that the rebellion would act as a springboard to rescue King Charles from captivity on the Isle of Wight. Under the plan, 4,000 to 5,000 Royalist soldiers, recruited from the area, would meet at Banstead Downs under the pretext of attending a race meeting. From there they would march from Reigate towards the Isle of Wight, raising troops en route.

Supporters of the plan included the Duke of Buckingham, his brother, Lord Francis Villiers, the Duke of Richmond, Lord Andover and the Earl of Peterborough. The commander in charge, Henry Rich, Earl of Holland, was a former favourite of James I who had supported Parliament in the earlier stages of the war. He was assisted by a Major Dalbier, who had himself left the Parliamentary army accused of incompetence.

The Earl of Holland was later attacked in an anonymous pamphlet published in 1648, 'The Decoy'. Major Lewis Audley, commander of the parliamentary horse, Clarendon, Henry Frierson, Anderson and Aubrey also gave conflicting accounts of events.

The rebellion was planned to begin on 5 July 1648. According to a London news-sheet, 'The Moderate', Royalist sympathisers left London on the day before the revolt, 'West out of Town by Water'. Arms had been supplied by Thomas Friar, a ships chandler in Tower Street, while horses were collected at Chelsea.

A large part of the rebels assembled at Kingston where, according to Clarendon, 'many persons of honour and quality came to see them'. During the previous few days, the Earl of Holland had been actively recruiting in the town, which was known for its Royalist sympathisers.

10 *Colonel Henry Rich, Earl of Holland, was the instigator of the ill-fated Surrey rebellion of 1648. An engraving by J. Themsent after the painting by Van Dyck.*

On 5 July 1648, according to Audley, six hundred horses marched from Kingston towards Banstead Down. But they were already too late for their rendezvous on the Down, and marched on instead towards Reigate, leaving a rearguard at Redhill. The army stayed the night in Reigate and left the following day with the intention of reaching Dorking. However the troops returned towards Reigate when news was received that the Parliamentary troops had still not taken the town as expected.

According to 'The Decoy' the Royalist troops marched confidently but without military discipline; 'with so great security and disorder, without scouts or rearguards'. As they marched the Earl of Holland issued a declaration: 'We do take up arms for the King and Parliament, religion and the known laws and the peace of all his majestie's Kingdoms'. Yet the Parliamentary forces, warned by spies of the rebellion, were well prepared, and Sir Miles Livesey had already arrived from Kent to lead the Government army.

As the Royalist troops reached Reigate, news was received that Reigate Castle had been taken by the Parliamentary forces. These included 400 horse and 200 foot soldiers under Major Audley and Major Gibbon. The unexpected news was received with alarm and confusion.

Changing their plan, the Royalist soldiers regrouped and began to march back again towards Dorking. On the way, they met a group of Parliamentary troops protecting Sir John Eveling, who had come to negotiate with the Earl of Holland. The Royalist troops fell into disorder. According to 'The Decoy', 'divers quitted their horses, the foot their armes, our waggons were overthrowne, divers betook themselves into the adjoyning woods'. The Royalist troops once again changed direction, marching north towards Ewell, pursued by Major Audley and Gibbon. Six Royalist horses were taken in a small skirmish in Nonsuch Park.

12 *Title page of 'The Decoy, Or A Practice of the Parliaments, by the Perfidie of the Earl of Holland.' 1648.*

In the meantime, Miles Livesey had arrived at the outskirts of Kingston, where he received some opposition from foot soldiers. At Kingston, Livesey addressed the Parliamentary troops, asking them 'whether they would stay, until more resistance came to them or fall on that night'. But they cried, 'As one man, "fall on, fall on" '.

By late afternoon, the Royalist troops had taken up positions on Surbiton Common on the plateau at the top of the hill. They organised themselves into three divisions, where they were fired upon by Parliamentary soldiers, reinforced by forces under Colonel Pritty, who had concealed themselves 'in the brakes and bushes'. Skirmishers 'played valiantly' but the Parliamentary army held back from attack.

The Earl of Holland led the first charge, of 50 horses. It was, according to Audley, 'as gallant a

11 Left. *Lord George Villiers, the Duke of Buckingham, with his brother, Lord Francis Villiers. An engraving by J. Ardell from the painting by Van Dyck.*

defence and as sharp a charge as I ever saw in these unhappy wars'. But the Parliamentary forces advanced from behind with unexpected strength. The Royalists were outnumbered in horses, soldiers and ammunition. Defeat was swift. Royalists fled from the battle towards Kingston. According to the author of 'The Decoy', 'no stop could be made of our running, until we came unto Kingston ... where we met with our foot who cryed shame at us, and threatened to fire upon us'.

The battle was a disaster for the Royalist cause. Frierson reported that 20 officers and soldiers were killed, the Earl of Holland was hurt, 200 were woun-ded, 200 horses were taken and 100 taken prisoner. Many soldiers of the defeated army were arrested at London and Harrow on the Hill. The Earl of Holland with 100 horses was later captured at St Neots.

The author of 'The Decoy' bitterly blamed the Earl of Holland for the defeat. Reasons cited included the youth and inexperience of the officers, the 'neglect of a place of retreat', the lack of ammunition, food and arms, the failure to muster soldiers from the districts which the army had passed through and 'the great neglect of all intelligence'. By parlying with the enemy, the Earl of Holland had 'decoyed into destruction' the Royalist army, which had received 'No commission or Authority from his Majesty'.

Yet the battle is not remembered for the Royalist defeat, but rather for the death of the young Lord Francis Villiers, brother of the Duke of Buckingham: 'A Youth and Tender Plant of Honour' as described by Clarendon.

According to Aubrey, Villiers died in a lane between Kingston and Surbiton Common whilst trying to resist arrest. Aubrey recounts how, his horse being killed under him, Villiers turned his back to an elm tree and 'fought most valiantly with half a dozen'. But the enemy approached on the other side of the hedge, pushed off his helmet and killed him. It was six or seven in the early evening.

Clarendon recounted how the body of the youth,

> covered with wounds, was carried by water from Kingston to York House in the Strand; and having been there embalmed, was deposited in his father's vault in the chapel of Henry VII at Westminster, with the following inscription on his coffin; 'The remains of the most illustrious Lord Francis Villiers, a youth of great beauty, the posthumous son of George, Duke of Buckingham, in the twentieth year of his age, valiantly fighting for King Charles and his country, received an honourable wound and died in the 7th day of July AD 1648'.

His tomb still stands at Westminster Abbey, and Villiers Road and King Charles Road are named in his memory and in memory of the monarch for whom he fought.

CHAPTER
3

THE PLEASURE RESORT

WHATEVER its subsequent reputation, 18th-century Surbiton was not known for its respectability. Seething Wells was renowned for other attractions than the springs, used to treat diseases of the eyes and described by Aubrey as 'warm in Summer and cold in Winter'. Woodward's *Miscellany*, published in 1731, described Surbiton in the following terms:

One Part there is adjacent to this Town,
Which by the Name of Surbiton is known;
A Private Place, long mark'd to entertain
Kept Mistresses e'er since great William's Reign.
When Ev'ning comes, out from the Garden Door,
Each takes a separate path to air his W...e.
One shall with black curl'd Spaniel beat the Fields
Or take the Pleasures that the Common yields;
Another to the Thames shall steer away
To see the finny Race both sport and play,
'till satisfy'd with Pleasure home they turn.
In Love they revel, and at Night they burn.

The *Miscellany* also satirised Kingston Corporation and the Dean of Chessington, 'Gigantick Priest, Goliath of the Gown' who was said to have preached a series of sermons about two sparrows held in captivity and sold for a farthing.

Surbiton's roads were improving in the 18th century. By 1750 the Kingston and Sheetbridge turnpike was established. The road led from the Thames at 'Surbton [sic], otherwise Surbiton Street' on to Godalming, and from there to Sheetbridge near Petersfield.

A toll road was also running by 1755 from Kingston to Ewell. The *Waggon and Horses Inn* stood alongside a gate at the foot of Surbiton Hill while a toll-gate crossed the road at the foot of Surbiton Hill near the fishponds.

A new turnpike was set up in 1811. This ran seven and three quarter miles from Kingston to Leatherhead over Chessington and Surbiton Commons, which were in the course of being enclosed.

New inns sprang up alongside the turnpike roads, such as the *Fox and Hounds* on Portsmouth Road, established in 1787 and the *Old Harrow* in Chessington.

Farming continued at Berrylands and on Maple Farm, south-east of present-day Maple Road. Part of the farm was leased in 1789 to Christopher Terry; fields on the estate had descriptive titles such as Pepper Bush, Barn Close, Bucklands and Hilly Close.

The local brickmaking industry was also important and a lease granted in 1742 to Thomas Noriss of Brentford and Nathaniel Wincuff allowed for a 'piece of waste in Surbiton Common near New Pond' to be used for digging clay and making tiles.

Muddy Roads and Wild Commons

During the 18th century, the area remained thinly populated. Residents lived mainly in scattered houses and farms. These included a house and garden plots sold by Anthony James, a London pewterer in 1722 to Josiah and John Stevens for £100. Poorer residents were looked after in workhouses, such as the house in Surbiton Lane, leased by the Kingston overseers in 1728 for one year. The house may have been the forerunner of Woodbines, adjoining the present site of County Hall.

Many of the former manor houses remained, including Tolworth Court and Copt Gilders. The Manor of Fream was bought by Christopher

13 *Rocque map of Surrey, 1762. The map shows Surbiton Common, Hook, Tolworth and Chessington. Chessington Common is also visible. Brickfields and fishponds are marked on Surbiton Common.*

Hamilton after the death of Thomas Hatton in 1746, and the Tudor house was renamed Chessington Hall. This was said to have included 23 rooms, a kitchen, a dairy and a garden with mulberry bushes. It was approached along Garrison Lane, then lined by a row of Spanish chestnut trees.

Hamilton shared the house with Samuel Crisp. Crisp, born in 1707, was an aspiring playwright, and in 1754 persuaded the actor Garrick to produce his play, *Virginia*, on the London stage. The play only lasted ten nights, and the disappointed playwright retired in seclusion in Chessington.

Crisp was a friend of the novelist Fanny Burney. Burney had known Crisp from her childhood, when her father was a frequent visitor. Later she described the journey to the Hall, 'along muddy roads across a wild common'; it was said to be a place of 'lame gentlemen' where 'everyone pursues their own inclinations'.

Burney wrote her first book, *Evelina*, at Chessington in 1776, which was later published to great success. Burney is said to have danced around the mulberry bushes at Chessington when she was told that the great Dr. Johnson himself had praised the book. Burney later became Mistress of the Robes at the Court, but continued to visit 'Daddy Crisp' at Chessington. Crisp was buried at Chessington Church; the memorial praised his 'Enchanting powers of brightening social or convivial hours'.

The house was sold in 1796 to the Penny family; it was pulled down and rebuilt in 1833. In 1851, the building was bought by Lord Horatio Chancellor.

The estates of Chessington Manor surrounded Fream. These had been sold by Thomas Hatton to Edward Northey of Epsom in 1742. In 1797 the estate was bought by Joseph Gosse, a distiller of Battersea, who died in 1812. Merton College retained control of Chessington Park to the east, between Filby Road and Park Farm. The college still owns land in Chessington today.

On the Eve of the Railway

On the eve of the coming of the railway, Surbiton had a population of little more than 200, a hamlet within the Manor of Kingston with little sense of independent identity.

Pre-railway Surbiton remained a cluster of buildings around 'Surbiton Street' near the *Waggon and Horses*. Close by stood the 'Elmers', known as Surbiton House before 1823, built in 1777 by George Wadbrook, a local maltster. The Surbiton parish pound for stray animals stood alongside.

Opposite stood Surbiton Place, also known as Surbiton Hall, a mansion surrounded by parkland which stretched to the river and further to the south. The house had been built by a local distiller, William Roffee, in the late 18th century; Roffee had previously owned the Elmers Estate.

After Roffee's death, Surbiton Place was sold to Mr. Thomas Fassett, who enlarged the house and landscaped the gardens with the assistance of Lapidge, a pupil of Capability Brown. The next occupant, the Earl of Uxbridge, expanded the house to make offices. The gardens were enlivened by performances from the band of the Staffordshire Militia. The house was bought by John Garratt when the widow of the earl died in 1819.

Surbiton Place was described in an anonymous magazine article written while Garratt owned the house. A porch in the fashionable Gothic style led to a conservatory decorated with painted glass. A wide lawn stretched to the south, bounded by evergreen, cedar and ilex, with views towards Hampton Court Palace. The park was ornamented with a dairy with windows of painted glass, a summer house, emblazoned by coloured glass armorial bearings, and a grotto formed with shells. There was also a boat house, with kitchen gardens, greenhouses, a coach house and stable block across the road.

From here, the Epsom and Ewell toll road led past the *Waggon and Horses*, to the summit of Surbiton Hill. 'Broad Lane' continued past White House, later known as Hill House, which stood on the site of Surbiton library. The house was already in existence by 1812 when it was bought

"This Gate hangs well and hinders none, Refresh and Pay and travel on".

14   The Epsom coach taking an alternative route along Moor Lane, fording the stream at the Bonesgate Inn. According to tradition, the inn's title derives from a nearby plague pit. The name is more likely to derive from the name of the keeper of the gate across the ford—a Mr. Bone.

15   Waggon and Horses, Surbiton Hill. The inn used to stand alongside a gate on the Ewell Turnpike. c.1900. Showing the original timber structure.

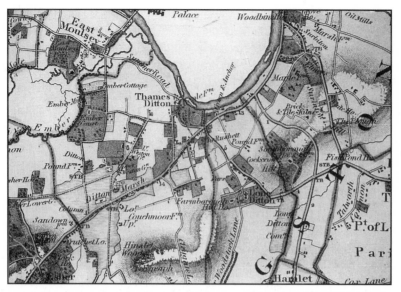

'A Map of the County of Surrey from Actual Survey', by A. Bryant, 1822/1823. The map was the first to mark parish boundaries; the Southborough and Hook spur is clearly visible. The Plough Inn on Ewell Road, White House, Maple Farm, Elmers, brickfields, fishponds and Fishponds House are all marked.

by Thomas Strange, a Kingston watchmaker, along with an adjoining lime kiln. Close by on the opposite side of the road stood a windmill and orchard. Another lane followed roughly the line of King Charles Road, and there were cottages in Middle Green Lane, later renamed Alpha Road. To the north-east stretched the 130 acres of Berrylands Farm and 219-acre Berry Lodge Farm. Beyond, as the *Surrey Comet* put it, the roads 'left the noble mansions of Surbiton Hill to cleave a narrow passage through common lands of wild beauty'.

Returning to the foot of Surbiton Hill, Terry's Lane led to the south-west roughly along the present route of Maple Road. The lane was unpaved at this time and lined by tall elms. The road led across Maple Farm, whose owner, Christopher Terry, had built a new house, Maple Lodge or the Manor House, in 1815 on the site of the present Claremont Hall.

Reaching the end of Terry's Lane, turning into Brighton Road, a traveller would pass close to Southborough Lodge standing in a large parkland on top of the hill. Built in 1808, the house is thought to have been designed by Thomas Nash, who went on to plan Regent's Park and design Buckingham Palace and Regent Street. The main drive ran from Ditton Road. The estate incorporated Southborough Farm, which stood along the wooded lane which became Langley Avenue.

First belonging to Sarah and Thomas Langley, the house was later occupied by Charles Corkran, an Oxford Blue for cricket and Improvement Commissioner. By 1851 the estate occupied 200 acres and employed ten men. The estate was sold off for development after 1864 by its new owner, Mr. Curling. But Southborough Lodge survives to the present, surrounded by suburban development on Ashcombe Avenue.

A turnpike gate stood alongside a barn and a group of cottages near the present-day junction of Brighton and Ditton Roads. The turnpike continued to Hook, which was a hamlet with a population of 189 in 1831. Hook was also an ecclesiastical parish, with its own overseer for the poor and surveyor. St Paul's had been built in 1838 with money from a bequest of £1,000 from the wife of the vicar of Kingston. Land for the church was donated by Thomas Langley, of Southborough Lodge.

Much of Tolworth was covered by the furze and gorse of common land. Chessington in 1821 was a small hamlet with a population of about one hundred and fifty. Chessington Common was a narrow strip of land on either side of the Leatherhead turnpike road. The enclosure of the commons, together with the arrival of the railways, provided the impetus for the transformation of the district in the middle of the 19th century.

CHAPTER
4

NEW KINGSTON

The Enclosure of the Commons

ON 18 June 1808 an Act was set before Parliament 'For Inclosing Lands in the Several Manors of Kingston Upon Thames and Imworth'. The Commissioners for the Act were Thomas Crawter of Cobham and William Neale of Cheam. Land was to be allocated in proportion to presumed access to common land, which included rights associated with the ownership of particular properties.

The Kingston Bailiffs were allocated land because they already held rights of access to Surbiton Common. Most of the land which the Corporation acquired at enclosure was sold to pay for a new town hall in the market place. One parcel of Kingston Corporation's land was bought in 1814 by Richard Galley, a Kingston bargemaster.

Enclosure gave opportunities for the wealthy to carve out new estates. Thomas Strange bought up

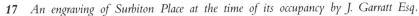

17   An engraving of Surbiton Place at the time of its occupancy by J. Garratt Esq.

KINGSTON INCLOSURE.

WE whofe Names are hereunto fubfcribed, Commiffioners appointed for carrying into Execution an Act of Parliament, intitled, " An Act for Inclofing Lands in the feveral Manors of Kingfton-upon-Thames, and Imworth, otherwife Imbercourt, in the County of Surrey, and for felling Part of fuch Lands for the Purpofe of providing a *Court Houfe* and *Market Houfe* for the faid Town." Do hereby give Notice, that we fhall meet at the SUN INN, in Kingfton-upon-Thames, on Monday, the 29th Day of Auguft next, at Eleven o'Clock in the Forenoon, for the Purpofe of receiving Claims, arifing within the Manor of Kingfton-upon-Thames : At which Meeting all Perfons having any Right or Intereft in the faid Inclofure, are required to deliver, or caufe to be delivered to US, in writing, a correct Account of the Property for which they claim, ftating therein particularly the Tenure of the faid Property; the Quantity thereof, with the refpective Names of the Occupiers ; and the Situation thereof.

Dated the 20th Day of July, 1808.

THOMAS CRAWTER.

WILLIAM NEALE,

FORMS for CLAIMS, may be had at the PRINTING-OFFICE, *Kingfton*.

W. Steader, Printer, Kingfton, July 18 8.8

18   Kingston 'Inclosure Notice.' Summons to claimants, 20 July 1808.

much of the newly enclosed land around the White House between 1812 and 1816. Charles Jemmett was another important landowner who bought land on Surbiton Hill from Thomas Sales, wheelwright, in 1825.

In the same year, William Walter bought 11 acres of land alongside Ewell Road and south of the future railway line. In 1826, Walter began to build Surbiton Hill House on the site of the present-day Surbiton Hospital, using materials from Kew Palace, which was being demolished at this time. Other houses followed, incoming residents being encouraged to build by what Biden described as the 'salubrity' of the site.

Chessington and Tolworth were also enclosed at this time and petitions were lodged in 1818. But enclosure was a long process. The course of roads across the commons had to be defined before enclosure was complete and 30 feet to either side of the public roads was set aside. Roads mentioned at the time of enclosure included the Tolworth Carriage Road, which ran from the *Red Lion* public house, Berrylands Road and Cox Lane.

Commissioner Thomas Tatham made the Tolworth Award in 1820. The enclosure of Chessington was completed on 1 August 1825 under Thomas Crawter; major beneficiaries were Henry Gosse and William Penney, who already held

19   Engraving of the first Surbiton Station, c.1850.

20   Surbiton railway cutting with steam train, c.1930.

Chessington at Hook and Fream Manors respectively. The enclosure of Kingston's commons, including Surbiton Common, was not completed until 1838.

The Coming of the Railways

According to Wyld's *Railway Guide*, the London and South-Western Railway Company was first proposed in 1825. The idea was revived in 1829, and a route was surveyed by the engineer Mr. Francis Giles. The initial cost was estimated at £1,200,000. Several attempts were made to raise capital; the Prospectus of 1832 offered £1,000,000 of capital in shares of £20 each.

One prospectus claimed:

No public work can offer greater advantages than this promises to yield to all classes of persons. It will afford certain and increasing employment to thousands of the labouring population; it will open markets for the whole agricultural produce of the southern and western parts of England; it will give increased facilities to travelling and commerce; and in realising all these important material and local advantages, it will secure to the shareholders an ample return on their capital.

The Railway Bill was put before Parliament in 1834 and received the Royal assent in July 1835, raising £1,000,000 in capital. In 1837, additional capital of £500,000 was authorised and Mr. Locke succeeded Mr. Giles as engineer. Later in the year, a contract was made with the contractor Thomas Brassey for the completion of the line between Wandsworth and Weybridge.

Two different routes were proposed, diverging at Weybridge. However, both lines passed through Surbiton. The initial route skirted the foot of Surbiton Hill, not far from where the assembly rooms stand today. But this route was changed in the face of local opposition.

According to Merryweather, author of *Half a Century of Kingston History*, published in 1887, Kingston fought off the railway scheme 'with all

21   Southborough House, Ashcombe Road, 1960. The house is thought to have been designed by Nash.

22 *Rose or Regency Cottage, next to the Methodist Church at 73 Ewell Road, was one of the first houses to be built in the area. Houses adjoining at 81, 83 and 85 were said to have been built to prove the value of local bricks.*

the values of old conservatism'. But the opposition of other interested parties was also important, including Lord Cottenham, who objected to the original route of the line because it would cut into his estate in Wimbledon north of the present-day Raynes Park.

The Railway Company gave in, and the line was re-routed further to the south east, along the present course. Once this decision had been taken, Kingston Corporation was happy to sell or exchange land which it owned on the route of the new line, including land at Clay Hill, and several fields at Lower Marsh Lane, which provided income for the bridge and the borough Almshouses. Local carriage drivers probably welcomed the opportunities which the new station would bring to ferry passengers to and from Kingston.

The new route meant cutting through Surbiton Hill, a major engineering feat. A drum winching station was built near Brighton Road to raise clay from the embankment to the Ditton embankment. Hundreds of Irish navvies were employed; they are said to have drunk at a new tavern opened at the top of Surbiton Hill, which survives today as the *Railway Tavern*. The first station would be a small cottage at the foot of the cutting, reached by a staircase. The halt was named Kingston by Railway and only became Surbiton station in 1863, when the present Kingston Station opened.

'Kingston' Station opened on 21 May 1838, to coincide with the Epsom races. The timetable for the first day offered five trains daily each way from Nine Elms to Woking Common. The journey from Surbiton to Nine Elms took 31 minutes. The line was opened to Southampton on 11 May 1839 and extended to a new station at Waterloo Station in August 1848. At the beginning first-class carriages were long and narrow with the luggage strapped to the roof. Second-class carriages had bare seats with open windows. Third-class carriages were simply open trucks.

23 *Hill House, Ewell Road, Surbiton, in 1898. It was formerly known as White House and was home to Thomas Strange in 1812. It was demolished to erect council offices.*

Thomas Pooley

The arrival of the railways coincided with the death of Christopher Terry, owner of Maple Farm.

Although the farm was close to the railway, few understood the potential value of the site. A single lot of about 80 acres was bought for the comparatively small sum of £10,500 by the maker of modern Surbiton, Thomas Pooley.

Pooley was a businessman who had come up from London; his family originated in Cornwall. At the time of the purchase, Pooley was prosperous, owning a malthouse in High Street as well as shares in three ships, the *Elizabeth*, the *Ring Mahon Castle* and the *Agnes*, which carried convicts to New South Wales. Yet he was not a member of Kingston Corporation, and had no reliable record of his age,

which suggests that he may have come from a poor background.

Whilst Pooley was not a gentleman he had close alliances with important local businessmen. His son Alexander was married to Jane, the daughter of the malster William Wadbrook who lived at the Elmers. Pooley was also allied to John Selfe, a tile and brick maker who lived at Little Elmers near the junction of Surbiton Hill Road and St Mark's Hill. Selfe, who was married to William Wadbrook's eldest daughter, Harriet, owned the brickfield and the windmill on Ewell Road. He also came at various times to acquire land to the east side of Ewell Road, the land now occupied by South Bank Terrace and the Shrublands Estate in Southborough.

Handsome Houses

Pooley drew the basic plans for a new town on his estate—New Kingston—which would serve as a monument to his success. His attachment to the project was such that he turned down an offer for £120,000 which was made for the estate shortly after his own purchase. He would have cause later to regret his decision.

According to a later legal document, New Kingston was planned to offer 'a great number of houses of various descriptions and sizes ... suitable for the occupation of persons of various means and circumstances'. There were ambitious plans for a corn market west of the station, railway wharves, a tavern, gasworks and waterworks. Wide straight roads were to be superimposed on the ancient road network. Railway Road would run in a straight line from the Elmers to the railway station.

Alexander Road, named after Pooley's son, would lead from the station to Brighton Road, whilst Surbiton Road would mount the hill to Ewell Road. Three terraces were to be built, 'Victoria Terrace', on the north side of Alexander Road, 'Albert Terrace' on the west side of Railway Road, and 'Adelaide Terrace' on the east side. George Street (Cottage Grove), would be laid out for tradesmen and domestic staff.

From the beginning, Pooley borrowed heavily to pay for building. The money which he received from loans was used to pay contractors who leased the land and paid Pooley an agreed ground rent. Pooley's first lease was issued in March 1839 to build a 'large and commodious tavern'. Later in the year, Henry Nottage agreed to pay Pooley a ground rent of £60 per anum for land in Cottage Grove. Leases were also issued to, among others, bricklayer

24   *Pooley's estate map of Surbiton. Shaded houses were completed under Pooley. The map shows how the street layout was changed after Pooley lost control.*

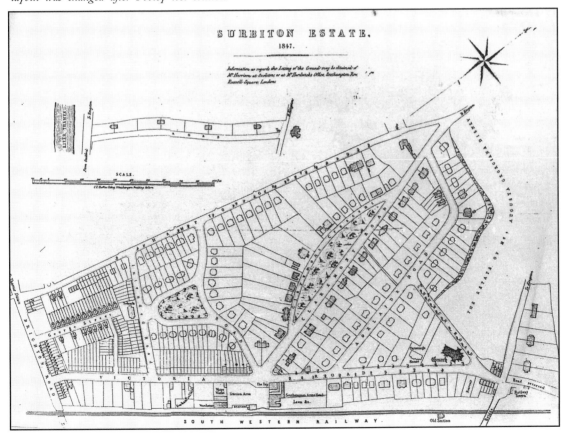

Edward Chapell, plasterer Thomas Thick and Robert Clements. Contractors at this received £22,400 in borrowed money. Pooley's creditors included Edward Majorbanks and Sir Edward Antrobus of Coutts Bank, Messrs. Drummond, Sir Claude Scott and Co. of Cavendish Square and William Wadbrook.

Work was well advanced by August 1840, when *The Times* noted that 900 houses had already been laid down, with 200 already built, some of them inhabited. Bricks for the houses were being made at local brickfields, probably those owned by John Selfe. According to *The Times*, the 'handsome houses, terraces, villas, Swiss and other cottages' would enjoy fine views, stretching as far as Windsor Castle and Harrow Church. The newspaper made no criticism of the style of the houses, later described by Merryweather in *Half a Century of Kingston History* as 'stuccoed villas, pretentious in design and capricious in style'.

The Times also commented:

> ... so excellent are the plans to ensure its success that there is no doubt of its coming much more rapidly to conclusion than towns of cities usually have done ... the value of the property has now increased to an incalculable extent ... the rapidity with which the whole has proceeded and the judgement by which it has been conducted, are surprising'.

But the article also noted that Pooley had met with 'considerable opposition' and 'prejudice' and had contended with 'a host of selfish feelings and interested opposition'.

The Times returned to New Kingston in November to report on the laying of a new foundation stone for New Kingston Market. The article expressed satisfaction that 'much of the jealousy which existed in some quarters when first this new town began to rear its head ... has subsided'. The new market, on a site alongside the station, would extend 66ft. by 151ft. with a pitched roof. The site had been leased to James Elmes, Professor of Architecture at the College of Engineers, who agreed to pay Pooley £50 a year in ground rent.

The Fugitive's Collapse

As *The Times* remarked, a charter for the new market had not yet been granted. It never was. In November 1840, a committee was set up by the Corporation with instructions to the town clerk to give notice to Mr. Pooley that an application for creating a market in the new town would be opposed. The committee consisted of the most powerful members of the Borough Corporation; The Mayor, Mr. Mercer, Mr. Jones, Mr. Nightingale, Mr. Shrubsole and Alderman Fricker.

In the meantime, Pooley continued to borrow large sums of money. £2,000 was borrowed in December 1840, £4,000 in January 1841, and £2,000 in February. In March 1841, Thomas Thick received a further £2,000 to finish his work, and Joseph Chapell received £3,000 for the same purpose. But the houses remained unfinished and rents remained unpaid.

Pooley was forced to borrow more merely to pay interest. In Autumn 1841, he mortgaged his share on his ships the *Ring Mahon Castle* and *Elizabeth*. Between October and December a further £16,000 was received in loans but, by then, Pooley was unable to pay the interest. Creditors in Liverpool were also closing in and the crew of his remaining ship, the *Agnes*, went unpaid.

On 9 January, Coutts and Co. served notice on Pooley that they would give no further advances. Pooley blamed his arrears on 'the non-completion of buildings and non-erection of other buildings'. In March, he lost his half share of the *Agnes* and in April the mortgage lender Gregory took possession of the houses in Kingston.

In desperation and facing arrest, Pooley proposed a plan to John Stevens, the architect. Under the plan Pooley would sell the estate to Stevens, who would then form a joint stock company from the estate, raising £10,000 to complete building work. Under the agreement, Pooley would receive £120,000 from Stevens for the assets, plus 20 per cent of deposits when three quarters of the shares had been taken.

The proposals were discussed and rejected by Pooley's creditors on 25 May 1842. Pooley's case was not helped by a report submitted by a building surveyor employed by Coutts to value the estate. According to the surveyor, the houses 'were of very inferior class, and built with such inferior and improper materials as to render it necessary to pull down certain of the unfinished houses'. The surveyor valued the new houses, on which £22,400 had allegedly been spent, at just £7,536.

Pooley had no option but follow the directions of the creditors, who agreed to provide the £10,000 to complete the estate only if Pooley relinquished control. Coutts agreed to advance £910 and Drummonds offered £46 10s. An agreement was drawn up under which the new trustees promised to pay Pooley an allowance 'not exceeding' £5 a week, 'at the discretion' of the trustees. Pooley objected to the terms of the agreement, and a modifying letter was prepared by Stevens in which the words 'not exceeding' and 'at the discretion' were removed. Pooley signed the agreement on 20 June 1842.

Pooley's position continued to weaken. In August he was arrested for shipping debts allegedly concealed from the Kingston creditors. From jail, he offered to sell the Kingston estate outright, but Coutts and Drummonds refused, arguing that the property was insufficient to cover his debts and had been fraudulently valued. An opportunity existed to make Pooley bankrupt, but this course was advised against by Parkinson, Coutts' solicitor, as it would plunge the entire estate into litigation and make Coutts liable to Pooley's debts on the *Agnes*. Instead, the creditors proposed to buy out Pooley completely. Pooley would receive the residue of £3,000, after all debts had been paid, plus an annuity for life of £250.

Pooley was released from prison on bail. On 9 November, the weekly payments stopped on the grounds that Pooley had practised deception about his other debts. In desperation, with no means of support and with his Liverpool creditors closing in, he escaped to Boulogne. Soon after his arrival, he was informed by Wadbrook that Coutts intended to enforce an 'absolute conveyance'. Pooley returned briefly to London and signed an initial agreement to prepare a deed of transfer. He sailed to Boulogne with £20 from Wadbrook, returning to London again by boat on 11 January 1843, landing at Greenwich rather than at London Bridge to evade his creditors.

On 13 January, Pooley went to the offices of the solicitors to sign the deed of transfer. This however had been changed in Pooley's eyes, since it obliged him to pay his Liverpool creditors out of the £3,000 which he would receive for the estate, rather than allowing him an extra £1,500 to pay his debts. Pooley also claimed that an enforcer, Edward Hoggart, had been sent by Coutts' solicitors in contravention of legal procedures.

Whilst he was at the solicitors, news came of his son Alexander's arrest for his father's debts, which was especially distressing as Alexander was said to be seriously ill at the time. Pooley refused to sign the deed under such conditions but was allegedly 'forcibly detained', a 'violent altercation' ensued and Pooley and the solicitor Wright were 'thrown on the floor'. Pooley was then allegedly forced to go with Hoggart to the White Cross Prison, but on his arrival, his wife and son arrived and pleaded with Pooley to sign the deed. 'Being in such distress ... and with tears' he returned to the solicitor's office, but still failed to sign. The solicitor then suggested adjourning to a nearby inn, *The King's Head*, where Pooley, who had not eaten all day, later claimed he had been 'prevailed upon to drink several glasses of spirits', which had been bought by Wright. Returning to the offices, the deed was finally signed. Later he denied the validity of his signature, claiming that he had signed under duress whilst intoxicated.

Pooley's version of events was contradicted by the solicitors, who claimed that they had taken pains to ensure that the deed was freely signed. The solicitors claimed that the enforcer Hoggart had left the offices after Pooley's arrival, that the arrest of Alexander was coincidental, that Pooley had suggested going to the inn, and whilst there had drunk no more than a 'small wine glass of rum'. They also claimed that Pooley had insisted at first on being given the £3,000 directly to avoid paying his debts, rather than receive half of the money through the solicitors, and half through the solicitor and Wadbrook, as originally agreed.

Under the agreement, Pooley would receive an annuity of £250 for life and £1,500 for his own use, paid directly to Wadbrook. Of the £1,500 paid to Wright as a payment for his debts, £5 10s. 4d. was left at the end of one year.

Pooley's Complaint

Pooley refused to give up. On 3 April 1844 he filed a complaint from his house in Oxford Street to the Lord High Chancellor of Great Britain against his bankers, also implicating John Stevens, his former architect.

Pooley alleged that the defendants 'formed a scheme for getting absolute possession' of his property, to deprive him 'of the benefits to which he was entitled'. He detailed a series of alleged frauds taking place within a general conspiracy. He accused the defendants of depriving him deliberately of sums of money, including the £5 weekly payment, and the full amount of £3,000 to be received on completion of the deed. He also accused the defendants of 'pulling down and altering buildings', thereby 'diminishing the value'. He demanded that the defendants make their meetings and account books public and invited them to acknowledge that the value of the estate had 'increased far beyond its original value' and 'was likely to prove extremely profitable'.

The response was submitted on 11 October. Bankers from Coutts and Drummonds along with John Stevens submitted detailed tables and accounts, with a systematic response to each of Pooley's accusations.

Among other points, they argued that Pooley had practised deliberate fraud by failing to invest the money raised through mortgages in building houses as intended, claiming instead that 'only a small part had been advanced to builders'. They argued that the deed of 1843 was a 'good and valid

deed' signed without duress and claimed that Pooley had been 'very irregular in his transactions'. They refused to comment on the value of the land, merely noting that 'up to this time the said land has not proved particularly eligible for building'. Moreover, they 'could not say whether the same was or was not likely to be extremely profitable'.

Any uncertainty on this point would soon be dispelled. The Surbiton Estate was clearly 'better effected' without Pooley's name on the title deed; it flourished without the opposition 'of certain parties at Kingston who will always endeavour to damage the property so long as Mr. Pooley is connected with it'.

Pooley might have succeeded if the houses had been finished on time to an adequate standard. Instead, he passed responsibility for building work to contractors of dubious standing, over whom he had little control. Richardson, in *Thirty-Two Years of Self Government*, noted that the estate looked 'dilapidated' whilst work was under way and the possibility cannot be entirely dismissed that some of the houses were deliberately built to a poor standard or vandalised.

Surbiton has not remembered Pooley; there are no streets named after her founder and no public acknowledgement. Yet his legacy remains, in the wide tree-lined streets and the remaining picturesque stucco houses in Maple and Claremont Roads.

CHAPTER
5

COUTTS TAKE CONTROL

COUTTS Bank officially took over Pooley's estate in 1844. The Bank reaped a rich reward from Pooley's collapse. By 1853, according to Richardson, land on the estate had increased in value from £100 to £500 an acre; by 1854, 'it could not be bought for less than double that rate'.

Coutts, with the help of Stevens, soon obliterated all traces of the former owner. Some of the houses were rebuilt, including Albert Terrace and all but two houses in Adelaide Road. The names of roads and terraces were also changed; Alexander Road became Victoria Road and Railway Road became Claremont Road. Surbiton Road was renamed Upper Victoria Road, then Church Hill and finally St Mark's Hill. Later in the century, residents of George Road were refused permission to rename the road in honour of the Coutts heiress, Angela Burdett Coutts. Instead, the road was given what was regarded as the more appropriate and descriptive title of Cottage Grove.

One of the wealthiest women in Victorian times, Burdett Coutts was also one of the most generous. Grand-daughter of Thomas Coutts, she inherited her fortune from her grandfather's second wife, the actress Harriet Melton, who had died in 1837.

Burdett Coutts became known as the 'Queen of the Poor' for her many acts of 'cosmopolitan philanthropy'. In particular, she helped craft workers displaced by industrialisation, including Spitalfield and Ayrshire weavers. Her celebrity was enhanced when, at the age of 66, she married her 30-year-old secretary, Ashmead Bartlett. A life-long Anglican, she donated the site for Surbiton's first church as one of her first acts of ecclesiastical generosity. She went on to endow three bishoprics,

and three more churches, including St Andrew's Church in Surbiton.

Pooley had always planned to build a church on Surbiton Hill, and the site he chose was donated by the new owners for the same purpose; Coutts also provided £1,000 towards the cost of the new building. The Anglican church of St Mark's would be at the centre of a new ecclesiastical parish carved out of the former parish of Kingston. This later became the self-governing district of St Mark's, Surbiton.

The building of the new church began in 1844. The architects were John Stevens, Pooley's former architect, and G. Alexander, who also designed other buildings on the Coutts Estate. The church, with seating for 590 adults and 130 children, with some free places, was consecrated by the Bishop of Winchester on 1 May 1845 under the Rev. Edward Phillips.

Land Deals

The completion of Pooley's former estate created commercial opportunities for owners of the surrounding land. These included John Selfe, who began to develop his estate on Surbiton Hill from around 1845, using bricks from his own kiln. According to Richardson, the estate was laid out with roads approached by grand gateways, even before any of the houses had been laid out. The adjoining Berrylands Estate was sold in 1851, the land fetching £500 per acre at public auction.

William Walter was another important landowner. Although some of the land adjoining the railway on Clay Hill had been sold to a Miss Forster in 1840, much of the rest belonged to William Walter. Walter

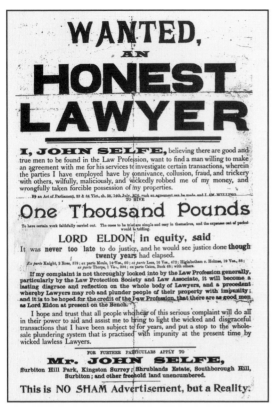

25 *'Wanted: An Honest Lawyer.' Poster placed by John Selfe, former owner of Surbiton Hill Park and Shrublands Estate. Selfe was still struggling to find an 'honest lawyer' after 20 years.*

had also bought Holly Hedge Field towards the fishponds in 1837. Walter was not always known for his public spirit and had caused controversy in 1839 by stopping up a public path on land leading to Ewell Road. The path was later restored.

In 1848, Walter leased off much of his land at Clay Hill to William Clerk on a 21-year lease. In the following year he leased more land to Joseph Erlam, who in turn sublet plots to William Clerk and Robert Churchill. Clerk began to develop the site in 1850, but became bankrupt in 1855. Much of the estate then reverted to Walter.

William Walter eventually destroyed his rival, John Selfe, in a court case which created a new legal precedent. With Charles Pressly, occupier of Surbiton Hill House, Walter filed a bill in Chancery to prevent his neighbour firing bricks, on the grounds that this constituted a nuisance.

Walter and Pressly won the case on appeal from Vice-Chancellor Knight-Bruce. In 1860, Selfe was forced to sell the offending brickfield and adjoining estate to Walter, who built South Bank Terrace on the land. Selfe lost most the remainder of his former estate gradually over the next thirty years, still fighting in his old age, when he distributed a poster around Kingston: 'Wanted, An Honest Lawyer'. Selfe was a ruined man when he died in 1899 with just £21 15s. 7d. in his account.

Another important landowner at this time was Alexander Raphael, who lived in Surbiton Place. A devout Roman Catholic of Jewish ancestry, Raphael was the first Catholic since the Reformation to become Lord Mayor of London.

Sudlow Roots, Raphael's doctor, later recounted a story which Raphael had told him before he died. While recovering from a serious illness, Raphael had seen a vision of the Virgin Mary, in which he was instructed to build a new Catholic chapel on his estate.

Work began on St Raphael's Chapel, which was completed in 1848 under Charles Parker. However the chapel was not consecrated, as Raphael had received a premonition that he would die soon after the consecration of the chapel. As a result, several consecration ceremonies were put off over the next two years.

Eventually a time and date for the consecration was agreed, and the Bishop of Southwark arrived for the service. When he arrived, the chapel was locked and Raphael had gone away. In spite of this, Raphael's butler let the bishop enter and the service was finally performed.

But Raphael's prophecy proved to be correct; he died a few months later.

After Raphael's death, the estate passed to his nephew who in turn sold the estate to William Woods, who started to develop the estate. By 1855 nine houses had been built in Westfield Road, along with 27 cottages; there were four houses in St Leonard's Road and five in Cadogan Road. Uxbridge Road and Surbiton Crescent were also laid out at this time. Within twenty years the pleasure gardens of Surbiton Place had disappeared. The Raphael chapel was closed for several years later in the century, but had reopened by 1908.

Seething Wells

The Seething Wells Waterworks comprised the largest development which Surbiton had yet seen. Land had been bought by Lambeth Waterworks in 1848, and work began in 1849. Work began in 1852 for the Chelsea Water Company on an adjoining site. Some of the land was bought from Kingston Corporation.

The *Surrey Comet* of September 1854 marvelled at the extent and ambition of work in progress:

> The banks of the river at Seething Wells are worthy of a visit, for the busy and animated scene there presented ... At the pace now maintained order and effect will soon emerge from the present temporary chaos and confusion.

The newspaper expressed satisfaction that

> ... in the congregation of such a number of individuals engaged in the works ... such small cause for complaint has been given on the score of irregularity or disturbance ... Above 800 men are now engaged, and over £1,000 was disimbursed last week for wages alone.

The newspaper was impressed by the insurance scheme which the workmen had organised in the event of accidental injury.

Water from the works was filtered over gravel for the appearance of clarity and pumped to a reservoir on Putney Common, from which it flowed down by gravity. Running water from the works was available—at a price—for households in Kingston and Surbiton. However, the poor could often not afford to pay for running water. A Commissioners' committee report of 1870 noted that, of 66 Surbiton cottages, 36 provided insufficient water and drainage. As a result, Surbiton landowners were compelled by the Commissioners to provide running water to their tenants to all cottages let at less than 9s. a week.

Parts of Surbiton were already provided with gas, but the service was improved in 1854, when a new public gas company was formed. Capital of £4,500 was raised to expand the Kingston works, and mains were laid as far as the post office in Thames Ditton. In 1862 a new gas main was laid down for Surbiton distinct from the Kingston supply.

Rich and Poor

Richardson noted with satisfaction that 165 'gentry' were listed in *Kelly's Directory* for 1855. Alongside the new Italianate villas were mansions for the wealthiest residents. These included Albury House, built for Mr. Dunnage, one of the Improvement

26   The first St Mark's Church. The central tower was an unusual feature in church architecture at that time. From a painting by Emma Shebbeare dated 1850.

27 *An engraving of St Mark's Church, Surbiton, c.1850. The church was in Perpendicular and Decorated styles.*

Commissioners, which survives as Hollyfield School.

The availability of countryside within easy reach meant that hunting was a popular pastime for Surbiton's gentry. Unfortunately, not all expeditions went to plan, as the *Surrey Comet* reported in March 1856. A large hunting expedition had assembled at *The Southampton Hotel* for breakfast. The party had continued to Hook Gate, where the stag was turned out. However the quarry became impaled on spikes in the river at Hampton Court, and the hunt adjourned to Epsom. Unfortunately

> ... the adventures of the day were attended by casualties, which, in one case terminated fatally ... another has resulted in a broken thigh to one individual, while other accidents, though of a less serious character than these we have adverted to, have inflicted a considerable amount of pain and inconvenience to those who unfortunately sustained them. We have ommitted to mention that during the time engaged in discussing the good things at the Hotel, some of the horses broke loose form the stables and ran wildly about the neighbourhood, inflicting serious injury on one or more persons.

Of course, not all Surbiton residents could afford to hunt. The vicar of St Mark's divided Surbiton into districts for the purpose of visiting the poor, and also established a coal and clothing club. A 'general depression of trade' in 1855 led to the formation of a Tradesman's Protection Society. The first meeting of the society was held at the *Railway Tavern* in April. Reporting on the meeting the *Surrey Comet* noted that, as a new neighbourhood, Surbiton 'presents facilities to that class of unprincipled adventurers who prey upon the capital and industry of the tradesman'.

Surbiton's wealthy residents depended on domestic servants. But long hours and low wages put Surbiton on the verge of a servants' strike in 1872. An 'anonymous cook' thanked the *Surrey Comet* for airing the servants' grievances, 'although I cannot see that much good can come from it unless some more definite steps be taken'. She went on to describe her working week and low wages, concluding: 'For all this slavery—for it is nothing else—I am rewarded by being let out one evening in each week from 7 till 9—a whole two hours—and on Sunday ditto.'

An anonymous correspondent, W.L.M. of Surbiton Hill, censured the newspaper for printing letters from aggrieved servants. 'What good the publication of such stuff can do', he wrote, 'I am at a loss to conceive; while the harm that may be done is very great in unsettling the minds of really good servants.' Another letter suggested:

Let good notice be given in the country of the vacancies, and plenty of respectable girls will be only too glad to fill them at far less wage than those who appear not to know when they are well off ... If the ladies of Surbiton are only equal to the emergency, they may, by actions like this, not only deal a heavy blow at strikes, but also by so doing help their sisters all through the country.

The contemplated strike among servants did not occur. However, local washerwomen did eventually take action against conditions and wages. An open-air protest meeting was held in June 1872 outside the *Black Lion* pub in Brighton Road. During the meeting, rivalry developed between the speakers from different areas. According to the *Surrey Comet*, there were cries of 'Long Live Surbiton' as a Mrs. Poulter ascended the chair, to assert that the 'will of the Surbiton women was as strong as the will of those from Norbiton'. The strike led to local washerwomen winning some of their demands.

Caught At Last

Even in Surbiton a criminal underclass lay beneath the respectable poor. A police raid on a house in Seething Wells occupied by a 'brother' and 'sister' was reported in the *Surrey Comet* in 1856. The brother apparently earned a living as a barber, while the sister bought and sold old clothes. However, persons 'apparently in a state of drunkenness', had been seen emerging from the house. Two customs officers, scenting wrongdoing, visited the house in disguise.

The officers ordered two herrings and a pint of porter. They were served by a woman known as 'Charming Sally' by the navvies, who 'very politely laid out the cloth, cooked the herrings, etc.'.

The two officers left 'after drinking several pints'. They returned soon afterwards in uniform. One of the officers was assaulted by a navvy, who was later arrested. Illegal stock was removed, but, as the *Surrey Comet* reported, 'Charming Sally, alias Augusta Brown, alias Augusta Lee and her "brother" cut and run and left the hair cutting and shaving trade, to be followed by others more fortunate than themselves'.

Local Government Before 1855

Kingston Corporation, with its ancient traditions was reformed in 1835. The Municipal Corporation

28 Albury House, later Surbiton County School, now part of Hollyfield School. Built by Mr. Dunnage, 1856. Photograph taken in 1931.

Act replaced the closed Court of Assembly with a body elected by eligible ratepayers. The new Corporation would have the power to levy general rates for lighting, paving, policing and other general services.

The borough boundaries were unclear before the 1835 Act. A report written at the time of the Act noted that the exact extent of the borough was 'not accurately known'. For some purposes, the jurisdiction of the Corporation extended over less than the Manor of Kingston, which included Surbiton, and for others it extended over the Hundred of Kingston, including Malden Richmond, Kew and the Dittons.

The report had recommended that the new borough of Kingston should be smaller than before, covering mainly the built-up area, including much of present-day Surbiton on the Kingston side of the hill. The report also recommended dividing the new smaller borough into two wards, Surbiton ward and Bridge ward. However, these recommendations were not carried out and three wards were created instead. The northern boundary of Surbiton ward was taken as the course of the Hogsmill river. Land beyond Surbiton Hill fell outside the new boundary and was not liable to pay borough rates. However, all residents of the parish, with the exception of Hook, were liable to contribute to poor rates, to pay for the upkeep of local roads, and law and order.

An Act had been passed in 1773 'for the lighting and watching the Town of Kingston-Upon-Thames.' Whether the 'town' of Kingston included Surbiton was unclear. An 1836 case submitted for the opinion of the Solicitor General expressed the opinion that 'those parts of the Parish called Surbiton ... were not lighted or watched' prior to the Municipal Corporations Act.

Under the 1835 Act, residents of the built-up areas of Surbiton could expect the district to be lighted, drained and watched. The Police Night Watch was certainly extended to Surbiton in 1836. But other services remained unprovided and the district at this time was later described by Richardson as 'a neglected, uncared for suburb, with bad roads and few paths'.

The Improvement Commissioners

In 1854 Kingston petitioned Parliament with an Improvement Act. The Bill proposed to extend the Kingston municipal boundaries to the edge of Kingston Parish, including areas between Surbiton

29 The Rising Sun Inn, *Clay Hill in the 19th century.*

Hill and Tolworth which had never before been within these boundaries. The Bill also proposed to give Kingston greater powers to improve local amenities such as sewage, drainage and lighting, under the provisions of the 1847 Town Improvement Act.

This was not Kingston's first attempt to extend its municipal boundaries to the south. The borough minute books record that in 1839 the Corporation had tried to extend the borough boundaries as far as Surbiton Common, incorporating the railway line. On this occasion, the attempt had failed.

Kingston had not anticipated the opposition which the Bill would receive.

In July 1854 a meeting of Surbiton ratepayers was held at *The Southampton Hotel* to register dissatisfaction with Kingston's proposal. Further 'stormy' meetings were held at St Mark's School, some attended by the mayor of Kingston, and an association was formed to protect the interests of the new town. With support from the association and Rev. Phillips, the Kingston Bill was defeated.

In early 1855, the Association of Surbiton Ratepayers put forward a new bill which proposed to give Surbiton self-government for the first time under the 1847 Commissioners Clauses Act. At the same time, Kingston submitted a new bill which, whilst less territorially ambitious than before, nevertheless proposed to incorporate the *Waggon and Horses* and the Elmers into the borough of Kingston. Sir Benjamin Hall also proposed a bill which attempted to address the grievances of Surbiton whilst maintaining Kingston's overall control of Surbiton.

William Durnford was employed as Parliamentary agent for the Surbiton Bill, which had received support from a wide range of local gentlemen, including Rev. Phillips, Charles Corkran of Southborough Lodge and Charles Walpole, a high-ranking civil servant. The proposal also received financial backing from Coutts Bank. The Surbiton Improvement Act proposed to give the Surbiton Commissioners the power to levy rates for the 'draining, cleaning, lighting and management of the district of St Marks', and included the power to 'remove nuisances', make general improvements and maintain the highways within.

The Struggle for Independence

As Richardson diplomatically noted, the majority of Surbiton residents 'did not appreciate the advantages offered to them by their neighbours in the borough'.

One of the reasons for Surbiton's opposition to Kingston's initial bill was the borough's perceived neglect of Surbiton in the past. According to Richardson, the people of Surbiton had contributed towards Kingston highway rates, but 'derived no benefits in return'. The Secretary for the Commissioners at the time of the 1894 Extension Bill, James Bell, estimated that only £100 was spent in Surbiton out of every £500 levied by the Highway Board.

Richardson also noted that Surbiton had no adequate street lighting until early in 1855, when

> a few lamps were put up in the Claremont, Victoria and other roads, and a rate of one shilling in the pound was levied on the residents. The lamps were few and far between, the light from each very small, and the inhabitants generally still used hand lanterns to enable them to pick their way along the roads at night.

Not all ratepayers and local interests supported the Surbiton Improvement Act. The Act was initially opposed by the railway, and the two water companies. Kingston also made several petitions to Parliament opposing Surbiton's Bill. One of the petitions expressed the view that Surbiton wished

> to impose on the other parts of the parish greater liabilities that they are now subjected to and relieve the owners and occupiers of property ... from contributing that which in fairness they are now bound to contribute, and which they ought in justice to continue to contribute towards the general expenses of the Parish, of which they form only a part.

This petition was signed by, among others, William Roots and William Wadbrook, an old ally of Thomas Pooley.

Public Meetings

On 15 February 1855, a public meeting, chaired by Charles Walpole, was held at *The Southampton Hotel* to consider the details of the Surbiton Improvement Bill. A second meeting was held on 9 March.

Among opponents was Mr. Feake Sandford, who took the view that 'No rational person would think of paving the district'. He believed that the provisions of the Lighting Act alone would ensure that the district could be lit 'as soon as the lamp posts can be put up'. He also cast doubt on the ability of Surbiton to pay for the scheme, since in his view, most Surbiton residents were 'persons of small independent property and persons engaged in trades, professions and public offices; residents who will forgive me if I say that they are not opulent and have no money to throw away'.

His views were backed up by Mr. W. Phillips, who thought that 'draining, cleansing, lighting and improvement ... were already amply provided for'. William Walter also opposed the Bill and offered support to the alternative offered by Sir Benjamin Hall.

In spite of some opposition, the Surbiton Improvement Bill was generally supported by ratepayers. However, modifications were approved, with Surbiton rejecting Coutts proposal that Surbiton should buy the sewers on the former Pooley estate. Coutts later agreed to hand over the sewers free of charge. William Walter dropped his objection to the Bill when it was agreed that the 15 members of the ratepayers committee would automatically become Improvement Commissioners in the first year without election.

Surbiton won its battle for independence. The Surbiton Private Improvement Bill for the ecclesiastical district of St Mark's was placed before the House on 17 April 1855, and was passed on 25 May 1855, Kingston failing in its simultaneous bid to incorporate the Elmers and the *Waggon and Horses* within its boundaries.

The first meeting of the Improvement Commissioners took place on Thursday, 7 June at St Mark's National School. The first Commissioners, under chairman William Walton, included solicitor Charles Jemmett, who resided at the Cranes, William Walter and Charles Corkran of Southborough Lodge. The lion of St Mark was adopted as the symbol of the new 'District of St Mark's, Surbiton'.

The first Commissioners were dedicated men, gentlemen amateurs who gave up a large part of their lives to public service in a manner which would be unthinkable today. Charles Walpole, elected Chairman of the Commissioners in 1857, served until 1874, when he retired from the Civil Service and left the district. Charles Corkran served for 27 until 1882, two years before his death in 1884.

Their energy was directed towards the improvement of sewers and roads and the establishment of a municipal identity. Today these issues seem mundane, but in the rapidly developing towns of Victorian Britain they were vital, even heroic measures of local pride and Christian responsibility.

Bones Gate, Ewell.

30 Bonesgate Inn, *Chessington, c.1900.*

CHAPTER
— 6 —

NEW RESPONSIBILITIES

SURBITON'S rateable population in 1855 was small. 286 individuals were rated on the north side of the railway, and 212 were rated on the south side, with a total value of £15,161.

To their credit, the Commissioners first made use of their powers in the areas of Surbiton most in need of assistance. Middle Green Lane had been described by Richardson as a 'quagmire'. The Commissioners laid a new road, with paving on either side. The road was renamed 'Alpha Road' to indicate that it was the first of the Commissioners' improvements.

Maple Road was paved and straightened in 1857, during the laying of a new water main from Seething Wells to Kingston. The Commissioners forced the water company to carry out the work at the company's expense. The *Surrey Comet* described the new road as 'one of the most commodious in the county'. During the work, an avenue of elms lining the road was cut down 'for public convenience'; their removal, whilst causing a 'natural feeling of regret' remained a 'matter of stern necessity'. Compensating for the loss of the elms, 100 limes were planted on the Ewell and other roads in 1860.

Not all residents of Surbiton were happy with the progress which the Commissioners made in the early years. A correspondent for the *Surrey Comet* of 19 September 1859 questioned

> ... why we are called up to pay high rates and taxes for police, gas, improvements, etc., when we are left to probe our way in the dark every evening if we have to be out at 9 o'clock? And why a policeman is most rarely to be seen?

The lighting problem was gradually rectified. In November 1859 improved lighting was provided in Berrylands. In 1863, lamps were lit during the hours of darkness for nine months in the year, excepting May, June and July. In 1864, 32 new

31 The six Chairmen of the Surbiton Improvement Commissioners. At the top: Sir William Walton. Following round from right to left: Mr. Richardson, author of Thirty-Two Years of Self Government, *Mr. Dickins, Mr. Guilford, Mr. Sumner and Mr. Walpole. From* Thirty-Two Years of Self Government, *by Rowley Richardson. Published 1888.*

lamps were installed around the new Christ Church, at a running cost of £4 per lamp, and arrangements were made to provide street lighting from 15 August to 15 May. In 1867 provision was made to light lamps for a further month, excepting only June and July, at a cost of £4 5s. per anum per lamp. Finally, in 1870, lighting was provided all year round.

Another problem to be tackled was that of drainage. Although sewers had been provided on the Coutts Estate, most of the district relied on self-contained cesspools. As the population of the district grew, so these methods of sewage disposal had become increasingly inadequate, especially on the north side of the district. According to J. Simpson, surveyor to the Commissioners, most open ditches in the district at this time were 'more or less polluted by sewage. The state of the whole district must excite great apprehension as to what may be its effect upon its salubrity and its future prosperity.'

Drains were completed in 1858 along Westfield Road at the owners' expense and Surbiton Hill Road and St Leonard's Road were drained in 1859. But the drainage of the Surbiton Hill area called for a large-scale scheme.

The Commissioners had considered several competing drainage schemes for Surbiton Hill in 1857. Cheaper schemes were proposed to dispose of sewage in the Hogsmill and Tolworth Brook area, but these were rejected on grounds of health. The Surveyor to the Commissioners, Mr. Simpson, proposed building a tunnel from a point near the junction of Tolworth and Ditton Roads to the railway bridge on Brighton Road. However, this scheme was regarded as being too costly.

The scheme which was finally adopted called for a sewer from Berrylands, across King Charles Road, along Browns Road to Ewell Road, along Leatherhead Road to the railway arch, and from there to the Lambeth sewer. This was a modified version of Simpson's scheme and was completed by his successor, Robert Brown in 1862.

The new sewer was described by a *Surrey Comet* reporter, who was lowered down a manhole at the top of Brighton Road. At this point the new sewer was 42ft. deep. The diameter of the sewer at the bottom was five feet. Brickwork lining the tunnel was transported into place along a rail mounted on wooden planks. According to the reporter, the atmosphere in the unused sewer was 'not unpleasant'.

The Surbiton Hill drainage scheme was regarded as a source of pride for the Improvement Commissioners, and an example to Kingston, whose own drainage scheme was not completed until 1864. The scheme cost £4,235, of which £1,733 was contributed by private owners. Charles Corkran and Mr. Curling both donated £500, while William Walter gave £250. The Earl of Lovelace, whose estate had been spared the threat of a sewer through Tolworth, donated £50, and the National Provident Society donated £225. Much of the rest of the money was raised by a general rate of 5d. in the pound.

The *Surrey Comet* hailed the Improvement Commissioners in generous terms: 'That they have vindicated their right to the title of "Improvement Commissioners" would now scarcely be denied'.

Unfortunately for Surbiton, the success of the sewer was short-lived. Brickwork in the sewer was damaged when new water mains were laid along Brighton Road. The Lambeth Water Company agreed to replace 75ft. of the sewer but work was not carried out satisfactorily and further damage was caused.

Then, in 1866 and 1867, the Sanitation and Thames Navigation Acts were passed against the background of a serious cholera epidemic. The Navigation Act extended the powers of the Thames Conservators upstream from Staines to London, and prohibited the outfall of untreated sewage into the river upstream of the Metropolis. The Act prevented Surbiton from discharging sewage into the river; the Surbiton Hill drainage scheme could not be used for its original purpose; the best efforts of the Commissioners had come to nothing.

Hearts and Minds

Victorian Surbiton, with its fine new churches and church schools, testifies to the religious commitment and enthusiasm of the age.

St Mark's, the first church to be built in Surbiton, was also the first to be rebuilt. The church originally had a central tower, but the low roof was said to make the building hot in summer. The church was also too small for the growing population.

An appeal for funds was made to rebuild the church with a new spire to the side, a much higher roof, an enlarged chancel and a lengthened nave. The architect appointed to rebuild the church was Philip Hardwicke. Sufficient funds were soon raised to start work and Angela Burdett Coutts made a private contribution of £2,000 to the fund. During rebuilding, services were held at the St Mark's National Schools and also in an iron hut against the side of the building.

By September 1854, the *Surrey Comet* was also able to report that 'Considerable progress' had been made in the rebuilding of 'this sacred edifice, which when completed will form one of the most elegant and commodious ecclesiastical structures in this neighbourhood'. The newspaper expressed the hope that the 'absolute necessity' or rebuilding would 'urge the completion of the work with the utmost alacrity ... should pecuniary assistance be required to urge on the undertaking, we trust the liberality of our neighbours will at once furnish the requisite aid'.

St Mark's reopened on Palm Sunday, 1855. The new church had seating for 1,015, of which 217 places were free. But the tower and spire had yet to be added. In 1857 an appeal was launched for the £1,200 necessary to finish the work and the tower and spire were finally completed at the end of 1860; a new organ was also installed. In the same year a turret clock was placed on the lower part of the tower at a cost of £303, bringing to an end considerable controversy over its siting; many had argued that the best position for the clock would be outside the railway station, where it could be more easily seen.

Christ Church

In September 1861 a letter was addressed to the Ecclesiastical Commissioners which put forward a scheme for the construction of a new church on a site on Surbiton Hill. According to Richardson, support for the new church came from those 'holding evangelical views'. Previously, evangelicals had worshiped at Hook Church, although prayer meetings had also been held at the London City Mission, a private house in Ewell Road.

32   Archdeacon Burney, vicar of St Mark's, seen here c.1900. He was born at Greenwich in 1815 and appointed vicar of St Mark's in 1870. He was made archdeacon of Kingston in 1879 and resigned in 1905.

A decision was made to create a new ecclesiastical district for the church, independent of St Mark's. Work on the new Christ Church, which would cost over £4,500, began in the winter of 1862 and the new church was consecrated on 13 August 1863, with space initially for a congregation of eight hundred.

The following eight years saw a continuous programme of enlargement. Funds were raised with fêtes and bazaars, such as a 'Fancy Sale' of 'Useful and Ornamental Work' held at Kingston Drill Hall in June 1865 and assisted by a long list of patrons including the Countess of Shaftesbury.

The first enlargement was completed in 1864, when a north chantry aisle was added. In 1866, two bays were added to the nave. Then in 1871 a

33   *Christ Church, Surbiton, in 1863. Engraving of the first church.*

south chantry aisle and porch were added, raising the capacity of the church to 1,204, with 209 pews available free.

St Andrew's Church
St Andrew's Church, unlike Christ Church, grew directly from St Mark's. The church developed from an iron church, costing £1,000, which the Rev. Edward Phillips had paid for at his own expense. This opened in November 1860 on land leased by Coutts. At the first sermon in the iron church, the Rev. Phillips outlined his mission to raise funds for the permanent building:

> How this prospective work is to be carried out is not now apparent, but from our past experience we may be hopeful for the future. Keep steadily in mind the work before us, the erection of a commodious and permanent church.

The district around the iron church was under rapid development at this time. The newly-developed area, according to the *Surrey Comet*, was

> ... inhabited principally by poor people, the majority of whom have not been inside a church for many a long day, not from any wilful neglect on their part, but simply from lack of the necessary accommodation.

With this in mind, the new church of St Andrew's was planned to be accessible to all classes.

A building fund for the new church was established following a meeting in July 1870. Most of the site was donated by Baroness Burdett Coutts, except for a sliver of land adjoining Maple Road, leased by Corbett and McClymont, who were developing the area. Funds were set aside to purchase this land, which meant that the church could be built right up to the corner of Maple Road. In March 1871, stakes were laid out in the ground to indicate the size of the future church. However the *Surrey Comet* reported that local children drew out 'all but one of the stakes' before the architect and surveyors had visited the site.

The foundation stone for the new church was laid on Friday 16 June 1871 by Baroness Coutts. A crowd of about eight hundred spectators turned up to catch a glimpse of the 'Queen of the Poor'. The church was completed in the following year at a cost of £6,851. It provided 760 sittings, all of them free.

St Andrew's was designed by Arthur, later Sir Arthur Blomfeld. It remains distinguished for its fine wooden roof, patterned brickwork and stained glass designed and made by Messrs. Lavers & Westlake. Mr. Lavers lived in Long Ditton but attended St Andrew's Church, and in 1888 donated one of the clerestory windows.

Work began on the tower in the summer of 1872, at a cost of £1,400. The tower was built as an offering of thanks to the recovery from illness of the Prince of Wales in the previous year.

St Matthew's Church

Work began on St Matthew's Church in August 1874, a few years after St Andrew's Church was completed. The church was consecrated in the following year. A new parish was created from

34   *A view of St Andrew's Church, taken c.1900.*

35 *St Matthew's Church, c.1910.*

36   The Surbiton Congregational Church on the corner of Maple and Grove Roads, c.1888.

areas formerly part of the parishes of Long Ditton and Christ Church in 1876.

Funds for the church were donated by William Coulthurst, a major Surbiton landowner, in memory of his sister. At that time, Coulthurst owned land in the district, including the Maple Road area. The church cost £24,000, a substantial sum, including bells and vicarage. The land was donated by Mr. Curling.

Coulthurst had low-church sympathies and appointed the first curate, the Rev. T.C. Griffith, formerly the Rev. Curate of Emmanuel Church, Streatham. Strict regulations were laid down by the patron as to the style of services. These stipulated that there were to be no full choral services in the church, that services should be quiet and orderly, that the choir should not wear surplices, that there should be no incense, that the church should preach evangelical doctrines and the Thirty-Nine Articles; and that the church should not preach any 'high sacramental views'. The benefactor also made it clear that the church living should be paid by the church congregation. Therefore, out of 800 total sittings in the church, only 125 were to be provided free.

St Raphael's Chapel

The Catholic chapel of St Raphael was the scene of two of the most glittering social occasions ever to have taken place in the district.

Claremont House in Esher was had been purchased by the Government in 1816 for Princess Charlotte and her escort, Prince Leopold of Saxe-Coburg. After the death of Princess Charlotte, Leopold married Princess Louise Marie Therese, eldest daughter of King Louis Philippe. The King, forced into exile in 1848, later took refuge at Claremont. The St Raphael Chapel was the nearest Catholic chapel to Claremont, and was therefore chosen for the marriages of Louis Phillippe's grandsons, the Duc de Chartres and the Comte de Paris.

On 11 June 1863, the Duc de Chartres married his cousin, Françoise Marie Amelie, the grand-daughter of the Emperor of Brazil. Children from the chapel school lined the approach with baskets of rose leaves and the ceremony was performed by Dr. Grant, Catholic Bishop of Southwark. Lunch was provided at the *Griffin Hotel* in the Kingston market place.

In the following year, the Comte de Paris married the daughter of the Duke of Monpensier, also his cousin. The wedding was attended by the widow of Louise Philippe, the Queen Mother, Marie Amelie, the English Foreign Secretary, and by representatives from many other countries. The *Surrey Comet* noted that it was 'easy to distinguish between the English and the foreign guests ... the French ladies generally wearing massive silks and costly shawls' while those of England were 'attired in those beautiful airy gossamer-like toilettes of the lightest possible fabric and colour, which to our notion are more suited than mere richness to such occasions.'

After the ceremony, the wedding party processed down Portsmouth Road to Claremont, where the wedding breakfast was attended by the Prince and Princess of Wales.

The Congregational Church

The Surbiton Congregational Church was founded on the initiative of Rev. Byrnes of the Kingston Congregational Church, William Leavers, and the Rev. Richard Smith. The first meetings were held in the Rev. Smith's house in September 1853 and a congregation of 40 had built up within three weeks. Later meetings were held in a temporary wooden building in Balaclava Road.

The new church opened on 27 April 1854 at a cost of £2,340, of which £1,000 was given by Mr. Leavers and £800 was donated by friends of the congregation. Within 10 years the church was too small, and funds were again donated by Mr. Leavers for a new church on the corner of Maple Road and Grove Road.

The foundation stone for the new church was laid by Thomas Barnes MP on Tuesday 27 June 1865. Under the stone was placed a brief account of the history of the church, a scriptural extract, a list of subscribers and a copy of a sermon. Designed by the Surbiton architect Arthur Phelps, the new church had room for 658 people, with space to build galleries for a further 250 at a later date. The original church remained in use as a Sunday and day school, as well as a venue for lectures and other events.

Sadly the new church was demolished in the 1970s after the congregation merged with Kingston. But the original church remains and is now used as an electrical warehouse, the foundation stone illegible with age.

Other Churches

A small hall with space for a congregation of 115 was rented as a Wesleyan Chapel on Ewell Road from 1861. In 1876, land adjoining Ewell Road was purchased for a new church, and an iron church was built on the site to accommodate 450 people. Work began on a new church designed by Charles Bell on the same site in 1881. Built of Bath stone with Leicester red brick, the building cost £5,660, the site £1,500. Completed in the following year, the church became known as 'The Chapel on the Hill'.

The present St Paul's Church was consecrated on 25 January 1883. It replaced a smaller church, said by the archdeacon to 'have had the appearance and style of a second-rate school room'. The building of the new church was supported with voluntary contributions of £1,500.

Other churches were founded in the district including the Oaklands Baptist Chapel, which opened in July 1874 and remains in use today. A primitive Methodist Church opened in 1879 in Arlington Road but closed before the end of the century.

37   *The Wesleyan Church on a well-wooded Ewell Road, c.1910.*

Education

School and church provision were closely linked in Victorian Surbiton. National Schools were built in partnership with each of the Anglican churches and relied on the financial support provided by the congregations of the mother church. This was potentially a source of deep frustratation and resentment by the nonconformists.

According to the *Surrey Comet*, National Schools provided the 'large and daily increasing labouring population' with 'advantages that result from sound scriptural instruction and a knowledge of the elementary branches of education'. The *Surrey Comet* expressed the hope that 'petty sectarian animosities' would be 'held in abeyance' in support of the schools.

St Mark's was the first National School. The school opened in 1848 at a site at the end of Cottage Grove donated by Coutts. The school provided accommodation for 40 boys and 40 girls. A master's house and boys' classroom were added in 1853, and an infant school was built in 1856.

Christ Church School began informally in 1864, in a house in Ewell Road which had been used by the City Missionary, Mr. Passey. The new National School opened in Alpha Road in 1868. On the first day, 42 boys attended classes between 9.30 and 12.15 in the morning, and 2.00 and 4.00 in the afternoon.

38 Regatta at Raven's Ait. Kingston Rowing Club held annual regattas from 1858. In July 1890 the first regatta was held which was open to all rowing clubs in the area.

According to the school log book, 'classification' of boys was made 'exceedingly toilsome by the thorough rudeness of the boys'. The ledger goes on to report that, a few months later, one of the pupils, Henry Woodbridge 'broke a pane in the classroom window with a stone from the outside ... His mother promises to send a glazier to mend it'.

By the end of its first year, the school reported an average daily attendance of 65 boys, 52 girls and 94 infants. Classes consisted primarily of scriptural instruction; holidays included one day set aside for the Kingston Cattle Fair on 13 November, and four weeks in the summer for the harvest.

Other Church Schools

The National School at Hook opened in 1860. In June 1871 a new school room was added. This was 30 feet long and 18 feet wide and was designed to accommodate 80 children. For its opening, the room was 'prettily decorated with flags and illuminated texts'. Mr. Ayre, addressing the children, expressed the hope that the young scholars would learn 'what the rights of property were' and asked for a map to be hung on the wall 'showing a plan of all public and private property in the neighbourhood, with a plan showing to what institution it is dedicated and the measurement, etc.'.

39 Yachting at Surbiton. The Thames Sailing Club was founded in 1870. Edwardian Postcard.

A Sunday School had been established at the Congregational Church in 1856. In 1862, an infant day school was added. The foundation stone for the first St Matthew's School was laid in 1879 on a site in Ewell Road donated by the Earl of Egmont. The school offered places for 220 children; the building still stands today.

Other Schools

Surbiton was well provided with private schools such as Melcombe House on Surbiton Hill, a 'High Class School for Gentlemen's Daughters' which offered classes in dancing and 'calisthenics' in 1879.

Mrs. Nops of 5 St Andrew's Square, under the patronage of HRH the Princess Frederica, offered lectures for girls and ladies in a range of subjects including botany, painting, drawing and piano. The school prospered and moved to Argyle House in The Avenue before 1887.

Musical practice was a source of much irritation to a correspondent whose letter appeared in the *Surrey Comet* of September 1872. Under the pseudonym 'Growler' he had the misfortune to be resident in a 'quiet road', which apart from a problem with barking dogs, was also occupied by a young singer. He wrote, 'It is highly virtuous in

40 *Mrs. Sterry who lived at Braemore House, Surbiton. She was five times Wimbledon singles champion between 1895 and 1908.*

the fair unknown over the way to practise instrumental and vocal music for four or five hours a day, but would it be too much to ask that she should do so with windows shut? The tones of the piano and of the female voice are alike beautiful, but one may have too much of them, especially in the various stages of cultivation.'

Self Improvement
Victorian Surbiton was alive with educational clubs and societies. The Working Men's Club and Free School was in existence by 1858, and offered a range of lectures in a small hall on Brighton Road. In the same year, the Surbiton and Kingston Horticultural Society met every month at the *Victoria Tavern* in Victoria Road. Other clubs included the Surbiton Tonic Sol-Fa Choir, associated with Christ Church, which began in 1879 with 42 members.

Surbiton's first reading room and library was established in February 1870 on Brighton Road. In its first year, the library gained 153 ordinary and 59 honorary members. According to the treasurer, the library was supported by 'many of the gentlemen in the area' including the Rev. Burney and Charles Walpole.

Groups associated with nonconformist churches included the Surbiton Temperance Society, set up in 1867. The United Kingdom Temperance Institute later established premises in The Avenue. The Surbiton Young Men's Mutual Improvement Association was founded in 1871 in association with the Congregational Church.

Surbiton Sports
Kingston Rowing Club began on Raven's Ait, then known as Messenger's Island, in 1858; the club later bought the island in 1881. Thames Sailing Club was founded in 1870, with boat houses on land donated by the Chelsea Water Company. Surbiton Golf Club opened on 8 June 1895 as the Waffrons Club; transport was provided between Surbiton and the site at Long Ditton. The club changed its name to Surbiton Golf Club in 1896.

Surbiton Lawn Tennis Club was founded as the Berrylands Club in 1881 on its present site opposite Surbiton Cricket Club. From the beginning the club boasted 11 grass courts and 200 members. The club went on to produce several Davis Cup and Wimbledon players, including Mrs. Sterry, born in 1871, who lived at Braemore House in Surbiton for many years. Mrs. Sterry went on to become Wimbledon singles champion in 1895, 1896, 1898, 1901 and 1908. Other well-known players associated with the club include Helen Wills Moody and Maureen 'Little Mo' Connolly.

Surbiton Cricket Club was founded before 1855, with grounds laid out on the north side of Maple Road. A rival team in early years was the local 'Indian Club', representing those who had returned from colonial duties. Later in the century, Surbiton was also represented by a hockey club which has become one of Britain's most successful sides in the present day.

CHAPTER
7

QUEEN OF THE SUBURBS

SURBITON was at its social peak. Italianate villas lined the new roads and the population continued to grow; from 4,691 in 1861 to 7,642 in 1871 and 9,416 in 1881.

Avenue Elmers was developed in 1872 by Corbett and McClymont, with land purchased from Coulthurst and Majorbanks adjoining the Elmer's Estate. Building work began in The Avenue in the same year. In May 1875, the Cranes Estate was sold for development by the Jemmett family. It was described in the Sales Prospectus as 'a capital family residence with garden'. The estate was bounded by Grove Road in the north, Surbiton Hill Road in the south and Clay Lane to the east.

In the following year, Corbett and McClymont purchased the Elmer's Estate and also bought land from the trustees of the Kingston Endowed Charities to develop St Andrew's Square. The

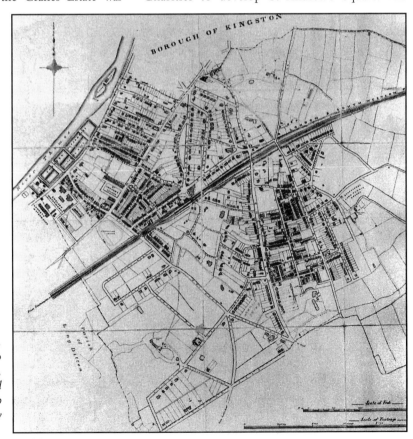

41 Map of Surbiton. Supplement to Thirty-Two Years of Self Government, *by Rowley Richardson and published in 1888. The map is based on the ordnance survey map.*

42 *Oak Hill Lodge, Surbiton, c. 1890, was the home of Arthur Bryant. Today it is the 'Sanctuary' office building.*

development of Maple Road continued in 1880, along with Cleaveland and Browns Roads, which was named after the owner of the brickworks over which the road was laid. Parts of the Southborough Estate had been developed in 1864. Building on the estate continued after 1882 when Captain Cundy bought the house from Charles Corkran.

As a place of fashion, Surbiton attracted some of the wealthiest magnates of the time. These included Wilberforce Bryant, Chairman of Bryant and May, whose family owned the British patent for safety matches. Bryant built his new house at South Bank in 1877, today Hillcroft College. The

house was designed so that the servants' quarters were completely separate from those of the family. His brother Arthur built Oak Hill Lodge in 1880. This is now the 'Sanctuary' office building.

The Bryant family was Quaker, and Wilberforce sponsored two 'Coffee Taverns' in Surbiton; the Spread Eagle and The Anchor. He also provided Surbiton with a private meeting house, the Gables Theatre, built in 1884 on the site of Bath Lodge. The theatre was used for plays and concerts, both amateur and professional.

Bryant left Surbiton in 1888, the year of the matchgirls' strike at the east-end factory at Bow.

Conditions at the factory were criticised by Booth, who found that many of the girls were suffering from an illness caused by excessive contact with phosphorus. Bryant's house was bought by Arthur Cooper, private doctor to the Prince of Wales. Cooper's specialism was such that, according to Philip Ziegler, the appearance of his 'clap-trap' outside the houses of Mayfair or Belgravia was liable to draw gossip and social embarrassment.

The Queen's Promenade

In their quest for efficiency and value for money, the Improvement Commissioners sometimes came into conflict with Kingston Corporation. A source of disagreement was the Queen's Promenade. This was built up with spoil from the construction of the Chelsea Waterworks. The promenade was financed entirely by Kingston Corporation, which had previously leased some of the land to Alexander Raphael, even though a short stretch lay within the boundaries of Surbiton.

The opening of the promenade on 27 August 1856 was arranged to coincide with a visit made by the Queen to Claremont House. Unfortunately the Queen was not disposed to attend the opening ceremony, but this did not deter the worthies of Kingston Corporation. On her return from Claremont the Queen encountered a barrier on Portsmouth Road, which necessitated a diversion along the new road and promenade. According to the *Surrey Comet*, which reported the story in January 1901, 'Her Majesty expressed some displeasure at the incident'.

By 1863, the promenade was in a bad state. According to the *Surrey Comet*, the surface was 'crumbling away' with 'gaps and fissures at every step'. But repair costs were high, and in 1865 the Kingston Town Clerk requested the Surbiton Commissioners to contribute a fair share towards restoration work. Unfortunately help was not forthcoming and the work was completed in 1867 without Surbiton's help.

In 1872, the town clerk again asked Surbiton to contribute to the upkeep of the promenade but Surbiton refused. It was not until 1874 that Surbiton finally agreed to contribute £25 per annum for maintenance; this was raised to £50 in 1886.

Roads and Recreation

Surbiton ratepayers faced increased bills during the 1870s and '80s. This was partly due to the closure of the turnpike trusts; the Ewell and Portsmouth Turnpike Trust, renewed in 1861 to pay off debts, ended in 1870; the Kingston and Leatherhead Trust wound down in 1883. These roads then became the responsibility of the Surbiton Commissioners, who also had to maintain an ever-growing road network. The increased cost of road maintenance was one factor contributing to a rise in average rates per head by over a shilling in the pound between 1876 and 1887.

The Commissioners did not shirk their highway responsibilities. Clay Lane was built into a public highway in 1867, with gravel from the Chelsea Waterworks. The north side of Victoria Road was paved in 1868 and four men from the workhouse were employed to maintain roads continuously in 1870. Cleaveland and Cadogan Roads were made public in 1866, The Avenue in 1868, St Philips' Road in 1872, Avenue Elmers in 1878 and Langley Road in 1879. The Commissioners also forcibly took over several private roads, including three roads on the Surbiton Hill Estate.

Some of the Commissioners' road schemes were frustrated by private owners. Work began in 1886 to widen Lamberts Road and the Retreat as part of improvements to the King Charles Road Bridge. But work was delayed when one of the landowners, Mr. Rastrick, demanded compensation of £160 rather than the £50 offered by the Commissioners. The case went to court, but the jury rejected Mr. Rastrick's claim, and instead ordered him reduced compensation of £42 10s.

Improvements continued to be made later in the century. The Alexandra recreation ground was purchased and South Bank, Browns Road and Glenbuck Road were widened. The recreation ground in Brighton Road was lost to speculative builders in 1888, but an alternative ground was leased on the site of the present Balaclava Ground from the Earl of Lovelace at a cost of £30 a year. As a consequence of this and other expenditures, the Improvement Commissioners were forced to borrow the sum of £5,000 in August 1891.

43   Surbiton Cottage Hospital, 1883.

Emergency Services

Surbiton applied for funds to build a police station in 1867—the same year as the station at Kingston opened. Surbiton's modest plans called for a cottage manned by a local constable, but the plan was postponed until the local population had increased. The plan was revived in 1884, but local residents objected to the proposed site in Langley Road and the plan was again postponed. The station finally opened in 1888, on a site in Tolworth.

The Surbiton Volunteer Fire Brigade was founded in 1863. A 'Roberts Patent Manual' fire engine was bought for £158, with a garage for £52. The engine, named after Sir Gerald Talbot, was kept on Fire Bell Alley on Ewell Road.

In 1879 Surbiton joined with the Kingston Volunteer Fire Brigade. The new steam engine was kept at stables in St Jame's Road and moved in 1886 to a site off Victoria Road now occupied by Sainsbury's.

Public Health

Mr. M. Coleman, Surbiton's first Medical Officer, was appointed in 1873 under the provisions of the first Public Health Act, which had been enacted in the previous year. He was succeeded by his son, Dr. Owen Coleman in 1876. In his first report, Coleman praised the general health of the district, noting the low death rate of Surbiton. Even, so, infectious diseases such as whooping cough, scarlet fever and measles were still potential killers, and a diphtheria epidemic in 1878 and 1880 caused a spate of deaths. Nevertheless, by 1886 Surbiton recorded a death rate of just 11.6 per thousand, compared to a rate in the London outer ring of 16.7 per thousand.

Surbiton's first hospital opened in 1870 at York Villa on the site of the former post office on Victoria Road. An appeal was later launched for funds to build a new hospital on a site in St James' Road. The United Temperance Association lent £4,000 of the £8,750 needed for the new hospital, which opened in April 1883 with space for 12 beds and two cots. Money was also donated by 300 private subscribers.

The closure of the Surbiton Hill sewer forced Surbiton to develop a new drainage scheme. The Sanitary Health Act allowed local authorities to combine with neighbouring ones and in 1866 Surbiton proposed the first of many joint schemes— a scheme with Kingston. Another plan was proposed in the following year in which Surbiton would take sewage from a wide area, and treat it by 'broad irrigation' over a large area of land. Unfortunately a site for this process was not identified.

Another combined scheme was proposed in 1874. The scheme proposed to dispose of all sewage from the Thames Valley between Windsor and London by building a pipe to the sea. But an inquiry concluded, in the words of Richardson, that the scheme was 'too heroic' and the idea, like

many before, was jettisoned. A further scheme in conjunction with Molesey also floundered.

In the end, Surbiton was forced to co-operate with Kingston, which had made a contract with the Native Guano Company in 1885 for works at Down Hall. Surbiton formally accepted Kingston's invitation to join the scheme in January 1887 and work began to build a new sewer to connect the Surbiton and Kingston drainage systems.

The new sewer was built by Messrs. Nelson and Co. of Cardiff, under the engineer, Robert Gordon. The cost was £8,000, to include a 27-inch cast-iron pipe 5,850 feet long and a brick sewer 2,220 feet long.

The sewer opened on 29 June 1889 and served Surbiton, but not Hook or Tolworth. A plan for drainage of these areas, proposed by the Kingston Rural Sanitary Authority, was rejected at this time on financial grounds.

44   Langley Avenue before development. Illustration from the Sale Prospectus for Southborough Estate. Nearby Langley Road was considered by Richardson to be 'sufficiently picturesque' to form a setting for a 'love scene' in a novel by a local writer, S.W. Fullom.

The Surbiton Station Petition

The inadequacies of the original 'Kingston' Station had long been recognised. An article in the *Surrey Comet* of 19 January 1856, noting the 'vast improvements' in the area, and the 'villa residences of a superior order' commented that the station was

> ... not only unworthy of the surrounding architecture of the vicinity, but in a degree inadequate to meet the requirements of the numerous passengers who daily have to avail themselves of its accommodation.

A new line was due for completion from Richmond to the borough of Kingston in 1863. For the first time, 'Surbiton' Station would have a rival. The Improvement Commissioners were spurred into action and a petition was sent to the

Directors of the South Western Railway to complain about the station. The ticket and waiting rooms were said to be too small, while the narrow platforms and lack of a first-class waiting room were also problems. The petition also complained about insufficient carriage communication between the north and south sides of the platform. 'The public are entitled to an improved state of things at the Surbiton Station' exclaimed the *Surrey Comet*.

As a result of the petition, some improvements were made to the station buildings, the platforms were lengthened and the waiting rooms enlarged. In the meantime the new Kingston Station opened on 1 July 1863, and in 1864 it received Royal patronage when Queen Victoria visited the Duc de Chartres at Morgan House in Ham.

45 *Surbiton Station around 1880. The* Southampton Hotel *is on the left.*

New Lines

Plans for a new line linking Surbiton with Epsom and Richmond had been proposed in 1844 by the Middlesex and Surrey Junction Railway Company. The Kingston Borough Corporation set up a committee to discuss the scheme, rejecting proposals to build a new station at Norbiton, and insisting that the line from Epsom should run into Surbiton. But the line was never built.

A new line was proposed in 1880 from Guildford to Putney via Surbiton. The scheme was backed, not by London and South-Western, but by a local committee which included the Earl of Lovelace, the Earl of Onslow and the Chairman of the Surbiton Improvement Commissioners. The plans called for a new line parallel with Villiers Road to Norbiton, and from there across Wimbledon Common to Putney Bridge, where it would connect with the Metropolitan Railway. The scheme also included a new bridge over the railway at Surbiton opposite to Adelaide Road, with improvements to the station.

Support for the scheme was demonstrated at a public meeting in March 1881. But the proposals were opposed by the London and South-Western Railway Company, and also by the conservators of Wimbledon Common. The local consortium backed down and joined forces with the London and South-Western and the Metropolitan Railway to build a line along the original route.

Work began on the line from Guildford to Surbiton which opened in February 1885. Some

46   Half-Shilling Butchers opened in 1843. One of the earliest Surbiton photographs taken c.1854.

sites along the proposed route from Surbiton to Putney were bought, including the Oil Mill in Villiers Road, which closed down as a result. Further improvements were also made to Surbiton Station following a formal complaint lodged in 1883, and work to widen the King Charles Bridge was authorised at the railway company's expense.

However, work never began on the line from Surbiton to Putney. In 1884 the railway company presented a bill to Parliament to delay work on the Putney line. Initially this bill was rejected in the face of local opposition and a petition by the Improvement Commissioners. But in the spring of 1885 the railway company made a second attempt to delay the line. This time the company was successful; permission was granted to delay purchase of land for two years, and final completion of the line to 1890.

By October 1885 it was clear that the Surbiton/ Putney line would never be built. The *Surrey Comet*

took a hostile tone:

> From the very beginning of this project, there has been nothing but bad faith, broken promises and procrastination. From first to last the history of the proposed Kingston and Fulham line has been an unpleasant illustration of how a powerful railway monopoly can overcome the most strenuous opposition, wriggle its purposes through Committees of the House, hoodwink the Legislators, and act in direct opposition to the wishes of the inhabitants of the district.

Surbiton never received its link to the west end. Instead, the Metropolitan District Railway Company extended their line from Putney Bridge to Wimbledon in 1887; the line from Surbiton to Wimbledon was also widened, leading to the removal of a row of pine trees at Surbiton Station.

CHAPTER
8

FASHION AND WEALTH

THE failure of the Surbiton to Fulham railway may have contributed to the gradual decline of Surbiton as a place of fashion. But social decline was not apparent in the *Illustrated Directory to Kingston and Surbiton,* published in 1891. The *Directory* associated Surbiton with

> ... the eclat of fashion and wealth and modern improvement ... wide pleasant streets shaded by luxurious trees; a splendid river-side promenade; handsome well-stocked shops; stately places of worship and good educational facilities.

The district was also said to enjoy an 'immunity from epidemic disorders'.

At the time of the *Directory,* Surbiton had recently acquired new assembly rooms. The *Directory* noted that these had been built by a private company, 'more with a view to adding to the attraction of Surbiton than with a view of making large dividends'.

Surbiton citizens had long been concerned about the effect of Surbiton's lack of public buildings on its social prestige. Attempts had been made in 1870 and again in 1882 to build a theatre and concert hall; at the second attempt, a site for the new buildings was chosen on St James' Road, and the 'Surbiton Public Rooms Company Ltd.' tried unsuccessfully to raise capital of £8,000 in shares of £5 each. A public meeting was held in 1887 to discuss the provision of a lecture hall or public library, but only £550 was raised in subscriptions towards the cost of the scheme, estimated at £7,000. Another attempt was made to raise capital by private means in the following year. On this occasion, 6,000 shares of £1 were successfully issued, and the assembly rooms opened in 1889 on the site of the former

Elmers House. The new building offered space for 800, a stage, a supper room and tea room.

The rooms soon proved 'a very fair success'. One notable event was a 'Tableau Vivant—a Dream of Fair Women' performed in January 1894 in aid of the St Mark's Men's and Boys' Clubs. The performance was attended by HRH the Duke and Duchess of Teck and their son, Prince Alexander. According to the *Surrey Comet*, the auditorium was decorated for the occasion with 'choice palms and other plants' and two anterooms were specially decorated for the royal party. The newspaper found it worthy of note that the royal party 'remained throughout the whole of the evening'.

The first Joseph Ivimey Chamber Concert was held at the assembly rooms on a Sunday afternoon in November 1896. The programme included a performance of Mendelssohn's String Quartet No.1 and Beethoven's D Major Sonata, with Mr. Ivimey leading the quartet with his violin. The concerts continued on Sunday afternoons for every season until 1903. Concerts by amateur groups were also held, and the Surbiton Choral and Orchestral Societies gave frequent performances.

Surbiton Residents

Census returns for 1881 reveal a prosperous community of gracious villas, occupied by prosperous families and their servants. Artisans and servants lived in cottages, but there were few industrial workers in Surbiton.

Spencer Villa in Adelaide Road was a typical residence of 1881. The home of stockbroker, Herbert Crossthwaite, Spencer Villa was shared with his wife, nine children, a governness, two housemaids and a cook. Close by lived two governesses who were looking after four children.

The children's parents were presumably living overseas at that time, as one of the children had been born in Calcutta, and the other in the East Indies. One of the sons of an army colonel nearby had also been born at Poona in India.

The census reveals that several other residents of Surbiton had colonial connections at this time. The daughter of John Fowles, an East India merchant living at the Avenue Elmers, had been born in Ceylon. Thomas Hare of 13, St James Road, was born in Java; his wife was born at the Cape of Good Hope. George Wilson, living at the corner of St James and Maple Roads, was a captain of the Royal Artillery with a wife, Luisa, born in Bengal.

Other places of birth listed included Stornaway, Inverness, Folkestone, Germany, Ireland and Cornwall. Less than a third of the residents in the Maple Road area had been born in Surbiton.

Unusual occupations stated in the 1881 census included master mariner, shipping clerk, artist and unemployed governess. Residents of Cottage Grove included laundresses, needlewomen, bricklayers, railway porters and shipping clerks, while a cowboy lived in Brighton Road.

47 *Surbiton Assembly Rooms, Maple Road, c. 1900. The rooms were built in 1889.*

Notable Surbitonians

Victorian Surbiton was associated with several well-known writers and artists. Thomas Hardy began his early married life in lodgings at Hook Road. Thackeray, who wrote *Vanity Fair* also lived in Surbiton for a time. Richard Jefferies, the Victorian nature-writer and mystic, lived at 2 Woodside between 1877-82; the house survives at 296 Ewell Road. Jefferies wrote some of his most famous books at Tolworth, including *Nature Near London*, *Wood Magic* and *Bevis*. The popular Edwardian novelist Percy White set many of his novels around a fictional Surbiton.

Lesser known writers included Eliza Rowe, a resident on Surbiton Hill, who wrote a fictional autobiography: *My life, or the Autobiography of a Village Curate*. Jane Dewhurst, who lived on Brighton Road, published an accomplished volume of poems with religious themes in 1857. According to the preface: 'She has not had a liberal education and for what is written has had recourse to the Bible alone'. She died in 1895 at the age of ninety-four.

E.M. Forster was born at Weybridge and set one his most memorable short stories, 'The Celestial

48 Jane Dewhurst in old age. She was the former cook to King William IV and author of Poems by J.D., *published December 1857.*

Omnibus' in Surbiton. A boy living at the fictional address of Agathox Lodge, 28 Buckingham Park, is taken on a magic bus driven by the Elizabethan writer, Sir Thomas Browne on a tour of heaven. Returned to earth, he later persuades the president of the Surbiton Literary Society, Mr. Septimus Bons, to board the bus. Unfortunately, Mr. Bons, failing to see the vision which the boy sees, fails to receive a return ticket; his body is found fallen to earth near the Bermondsey gasworks. The story contains a memorable description of the Surbiton railway cutting—'that wonderful cutting which has drawn to itself the whole beauty of Surbiton, and clad itself, like any alpine valley, with the glory of the fir and the silver birch and the primrose'.

Local artists included Stanley Berkeley who died at his home in Hook in 1909. Unknown today, he became celebrated during his lifetime with animal paintings and battle scenes such as *Gordons and Greys to the Front*. He also produced an equestrian portrait of King Edward VII.

Sir Adolf Zimmern who lived with his father at Oakdene House, co-founded the Geneva School of International Studies and became educational counsellor to the president of the American International College.

Dr. Barnardo, the famous philanthropist, lived in Surbiton later in his life, although according to the *Surrey Comet* he took little part in local affairs, and suffered from serious heart problems in his last years. His house, St Leonard's Lodge, overlooked the river at the corner of St Leonard's Road and Portsmouth Road on a site now occupied by flats. He died in Surbiton in 1905.

A Darker Side

In August 1890 the *Surrey Comet* noted a general reduction of pauperism in the district. Yet there were still pockets of extreme poverty, as a *Surrey Comet* reporter discovered in June 1891.

> Surbiton is generally recognised as a wealthy and fashionable suburb ... nevertheless it is a fact that Surbiton has its shadowy side, and to anyone who cares to struggle to the terminus of a rough and muddy thoroughfare known as Marsh Lane, situate on the borders of the parish, would be revealed a phase of human life which would compare unfavourably with many of the dark spots in the Metropolis. There, under one of the railway arches along the main line, a family, consisting of husband, wife and five little children, is existing, Heaven knows how, but with a roughly improvised awning for shelter and in the midst of squalor, wretchedness and degradation. As for sanitary arrangements, no signs of such are anywhere visible, and the only means of obtaining a water supply is a hole dug close by, wherein drains the surface water. The five little children, whose ages range from two to six or seven, and who huddle together and cower at the approach of strangers, look lost in filth and rage—a faithful counterpart of the parents. The interior of the 'home'—a misnomer indeed—presents a wretched appearance, and only contains a heap of dirty straw mattress and rags.

The eldest daughter had apparently fled from her father in order to escape from having to work as a prostitute and was taken in by a Church of

49 *Admiral Jellicoe (1859-1935). Sir John Jellicoe became Supreme Commander of the Home Fleets during the First World War. He frequently visited his father, Captain John Jellicoe, who lived at Frampton House, Catherine Road, now the site of Ashleigh Court. The admiral's father died in September 1914 at ninety.*

50 *Monsieur George Pigache, seen here with his family, was the supervisor of the Café Royal kitchens in Regent Street, and the son-in-law of Daniel Nicols, founder of the Café Royal, who lived at Regent House in Berrylands. According to the* Café Royal, Ninety Years of Bohemia *by Guy Deghy and Keith Waterhouse, published in 1955, M. Pigache was said to be so fat that he travelled every day to Surbiton Station in a special cart. He died in May 1898, aged 47 and weighing 36 stone.*

England's Young Women's Rescue Home on the south coast; the father was demanding his daughter back, as the family had no other source of income.

It would have been easy for a Surbiton girl from a poor background to fall into prostitution at this time. The *Surrey Comet* of 22 September 1883 complained about 'disgraceful nightly scenes by disorderly females in Portsmouth Road'. The streets were also plagued by beggars; the *Surbiton Review* complained in 1889 about 'numerous whining able bodied beggars' on Ewell Road.

The Kingston Extension Bill
Kingston had not forgotten its failed attempt to gain control over Surbiton. In 1894 the borough made a new attempt to wrest control of Surbiton from the Improvement Commissioners. The petition, issued on 19 June 1894, proposed to include Surbiton and the Rural Sanitary District of Hook (including the detached district of Southborough) within new borough boundaries. It described Surbiton's independence as an 'anomaly in local government, which has been the cause of much friction and unnecessary subdivision'. A separate attempt was also made at this time to win control of Malden and Coombe.

Once again Surbiton fought back, using clauses in the 1888 Local Government Act which made it possible for local authorities to reconstitute themselves as Urban District Authorities. These were entitled to hold many of the powers previously held by church vestries, including the administration of parish charities and the collection of the Poor Rate. The new authorities were also democratically accountable to the electorate of the district.

Surbiton was anxious at the prospect of losing its hard-won sense of civic identity. H. Judd of Surbiton Hill summed up the views of many in a letter to the *Surrey Comet* in July 1894:

> We have waited long for popular government in Surbiton and now just as the Local Government Act places it within our reach, Kingston wants to 'absorb' us. I dislike this unification, I look upon it as an attempt to destroy our young municipal life.

A further problem identified by Surbiton was related to the distribution of seats within the proposed merged borough; the ward structure originally proposed meant that Surbiton could always be outvoted. Rates in Kingston were also higher than those in Surbiton. In the three years ending March 1895, Kingston's average total rate of 5s. in the pound compared to Surbiton's rate of 3s. 10d. Surbiton was concerned that the district's resources would be used to pay for schemes of benefit only to Kingston, such as the 'Back Lanes' slum area and the widening of Kingston's old roads. However, Kingston tried to respond to these concerns by proposing a scheme for differential rating between the two districts if the scheme went ahead.

The controversy fuelled old rivalry. Even Rev. Burney of St Mark's was criticised for writing a letter to the *Surrey Comet* which praised co-operation between voluntary schools in the Kingston Parish. The archdeacon was forced to

51 *Members of the Stickley family after a shoot, with hunting dogs and game. John Stickley lived at Sefton Villas, Hook, his brother Charles at Bankfield, Hook Road. Photograph taken c.1900 at the* North Star Inn, *Hook.*

52 Left. *Prize carthorses of John James Stickley in Hook Road. Photograph* c.*1900.*

53 Below. *The top of Ewell Road, c.1900. Oak Hill Cresent is on the right.* The Plough *pub used to occupy a site on the left, close to the* New Prince *pub. The row of buildings to the right of the picture still remains; the gabled building on the right is now a pharmacist; the parade of shops on the further left is occupied by The Piano Workshop. Original postcard.*

*54 Victoria Road, c.1890.
M. Griggs, milliners and fancy
drapers, stood on the corner to the
right.*

write to the newspaper to emphasise his strong
opposition to the merger, whilst offering his support
towards 'anything that tends to break down the
narrow parochial isolation which sometimes exists
... such as promotion of voluntary schools'.

One option considered by Surbiton was a
defensive merger with Long Ditton, Thames Ditton
and Esher. Mr. Bulmer Howell, remarking on these
proposals at a vestry meeting in July 1894, was
moved to comment: 'My private impression is that
they want to be amalgamated with us to escape
being connected with Kingston'. He went on to
express himself lightly in verse:

> We should not love Ditton so much
> Loathed was not Kingston the more.

Surbiton later scaled-down its plans to
incorporate the whole of Long Ditton. The Parish
Council of Hook had already agreed to join
Surbiton as part of the district of Southborough at
a vote in July 1894.

Kingston v Surbiton

On 13 June 1894, a meeting was held between
representatives of Kingston Corporation and the
Surbiton Improvement Commissioners. Kingston's
view was that Surbiton was trying to 'evade its
responsibilities towards the older and less favoured
part of the Borough'. There certainly remained a
major difference in the rateable values of the two
areas; Surbiton's value per head was £10 10s.,
compared to just £4 10s. for Kingston.

Kingston had a strong ally in the *Surrey Comet*.
The newspaper ran a series of articles under the
heading 'Greater Kingston' as the Government
Inquiry into the proposals began. The partisan tone
of the newspaper led to the Improvement
Commissioners refusing to place a record of their
annual accounts in the newspaper. This attempt 'to
strike at an editor through the pocket of the
proprietor of the paper' was described as 'a
particularly mean and futile act'.

In defence of Kingston, the *Surrey Comet* noted
that many of those who worked in Kingston lived
in Surbiton, including even such high-ranking
officials as the borough recorder. The article also
noted confusion between the boundaries of Kingston
and Surbiton:

> Of that dividing line many ... are apparently
> quite ignorant, calling Surbiton their place of
> residence, whereas they live really in Kingston.

The newspaper concluded:

> These instances afford evidence of the
> 'oneness' of the parish ... The ideal of true
> municipal Government should be to complete
> this 'oneness' that in the one community there
> should be a single governing body.

Kingston Corporation outlined its case in a
letter to the Surbiton Commissioners. Advantages
for Surbiton in the proposed merger would include
electricity from the new Down Hall works 'at a
comparatively small outlay of additional capital upon

55   Adelaide Road, Surbiton, c.1927.

56   *The junction of Portsmouth Road and Uxbridge Road, c.1927. The post box still stands on the corner, but the terrace on the right was destroyed by a V1 during the Second World War. The pillar just to the left of the man's head on the bicycle is also still standing, but Westergate House behind has been replaced with flats.*

57   *A cornfield on Ewell Road, Tolworth, which Richard Jefferies and Edward Thomas would have recognised. Photograph taken c.1900.*

mains and generating plant'. Efficiencies could be made in the number of officials, in providing water and police services over a wider area, in the provision of a public library and swimming pool and in the use of the Isolation Hospital at Tolworth. The merged authority would also find it easier to raise loans.

The letter concluded that a 'strange mis-apprehension' existed in regard to Surbiton's position. 'Obviously, it must stand to reason that not only will the ratepayers of Surbiton, through their direct representatives, still retain control over Surbiton affairs, but their co-operation with their neighbours on one powerful and combined council will render that control more effective'.

The Improvement Commissioners replied to these arguments in another public letter, dated 1 November 1894. Among other points, the letter presented the opinion that proposed public baths in Kingston were 'inconvenient of access' to Surbiton, while on the issue of establishing a public library for Surbiton, the letter declared: 'There has been no demand for this, but when the ratepayers desire it, the Commissioners are prepared to establish one'.

The Inquiry

An Inquiry into the Kingston Extension Scheme by the Local Government Board opened at the Assize Courts in December 1894. Mr. Bidder QC and Mr. Cripps QC appeared for Kingston

Corporation, Mr. Balfour Browne QC and Mr. Baggallay appeared for Surbiton.

The mayor of Kingston, examined by Mr. Cripps QC, reiterated the many existing links between Surbiton and Kingston. According to the mayor, the Queen's Promenade was 'chiefly used by Surbiton people' even though the majority of the subscriptions came from Kingston. The mayor also listed the other amenities which were paid for by Kingston, yet were used by Surbiton residents.

One of the most effective witnesses for Surbiton was Robert Gordon, who had been the engineer in charge of the sewage pipe between Kingston and Surbiton between 1888 and 1889. Cross-examined by Bidder QC he noted that 'very great improvements had been made with regard to house drainage in Surbiton'. He said that during the construction of the sewer, he had seen 70 of the Kingston sewers and house drains 'and the condition of them all without exception was most abominable'.

Surbiton's key witness was Thomas Guilford, Chairman of the Improvement Commissioners and also a major property owner. During the cross-examination by Bidder QC, Guilford described the advantages which the Commissioners had brought to Surbiton. He mentioned the Cottage Hospital, erected by public subscription, the assembly rooms and 'the best train service out of London, with the largest number of first-class station ticket holders on the South Western Railway'. The development of Surbiton, in his view, had never been assisted in the slightest degree by Kingston.

Some of Guilford's views were unreliable. He claimed that he could count on his fingers the people who carried on their business in Kingston and resided in Surbiton. He thought that Kingston library was 'not used to any extent by Surbiton people' and expressed the opinion that the majority of people in Surbiton shopped, not at Kingston, but at the stores in London. In saying this, he contradicted a quip made a few minutes previously, in which he had questioned how Kingston's shopkeepers would manage without the custom of Surbiton residents.

According to Guilford, to share in the privilege of the market at Kingston would 'not be worth a penny to Surbiton'. He felt that participation with

Kingston in the Isolation Hospital scheme would be more of a disadvantage than an advantage to Surbiton, since it would mean infectious cases travelling through the borough. He was aware that Kingston had promised Surbiton differential rating, but in his opinion this would mean 'differential spending'. Guilford's general views were all the more questionable in view of his position as Chairman of the Board of Governors of both the Tiffin Schools and the Kingston Grammar School.

Guilford's case was rested by Bidder, who tore angrily into him:

> Your case is that you are well-to-do residential people carrying on business chiefly in London, and you leave Kingston to provide the accommodation for the industrial classes with free libraries and all that is wanted now-a-days, and to bear the burden of that while you are happily free of it?

'Not at all', replied Guilford.

Kingston lost the case. The first meeting of the Surbiton District Council was held on 31 December 1894, fulfilling Thomas Guilford's boast: 'We are going out as Commissioners, and shall return as District Councillors'. The Bill was ratified by Parliament later in 1895, when the addition of Tolworth was confirmed.

Victorian Tolworth

Tolworth Court Manor had been bought by Lord Egmont from Nathaniel Polhill, MP for Southwark, in 1835. It remained in Lord Egmont's possession until his death in 1897, when it was sold for development to Stephen Kavanagh.

The Manor House was described by Brayley in 1850 as having 'long ago descended into a mere farm house with its usual appendages'. The house survived a serious fire in 1873 which received attention from seven or eight fire brigades; the fire was started by a vagrant sleeping in a hay rick. The adjoining barn, which survived until the 4th September 1969, was described by Richard Jefferies in *Nature Near London* as 'a great red roof' which rose high above the hedges, the line of its ridge 'seen every way through the trees'.

A population of 464 in 1871 had risen to 2,458 by the turn of the century. Some of the residents of Tolworth worked at the brickworks in Red Lion

58   *The congregation on the way to St Mary's Church, Chessington in 1900.*

Lane, which opened at Fullers Farm in 1874. Others continued to work on the land.

The poet Edward Thomas, who wrote a biography of Jefferies, gave a lyrical description of Tolworth at the turn of the century. The wood of 'scotch and spruce fir, hornbeam, birch and ash' had vanished, where Jefferies once watched 'dove and pigeon, cuckoo, nightingale, sedgewarbler and missel-thrush'. But the nearby view remained unchanged: 'Squares of plough land, marigolds, grass, stubble and mustard succeed one another in Autumn ... except on a few Saturdays and Sundays, this is a deep quiet country, even now'.

Tolworth Hospital

Tolworth Hospital was first proposed by the Kingston Rural Sanitary Authority. The scheme was fiercely fought by local landowners, including Lord Egmont, Lord Lovelace and the Liberal Land Corporation, who threatened to claim damages of £10,000 if the scheme went ahead.

But the Rural Sanitary Authority won, and the Surbiton Commissioners agreed to contribute to the running costs. The hospital opened in 1889 with 22 beds, for patients with fevers and infectious diseases. An extension was opened in 1906 with a laundry block and observation ward.

A Rural Backwater

Chessington retained its rural quiet as the development of Tolworth began. The church was restored in 1854 with a new shingle spire and flint exterior walls to replace green plaster. The south aisle was added in 1870. Much of the impetus for the restoration came from the Rev. Chetwynd Stapylton. Appointed curate in 1850, he later set up an iron church in Malden Rushett and walked the parish to hold cottage meetings weekly in Chessington and Malden Rushett. 'It was not unpleasant', he wrote,

> except when the night was rough and stormy, to have a walk of 14 miles out and home to hold these meetings; and I have always found a full reward in the well-filled rooms and attentive and sympathising hearers.

CHAPTER
9

EDWARDIAN SURBITON

IN January 1901 Surbiton mourned for Queen Victoria. According to the *Surrey Comet*,

> bells were tolled from the churches of St Mark's, St Andrews and St Matthews ... Shutters are in position on almost every business establishment, several flags are flying at half mast and deep or patriotic mourning is generally worn.

Plans were made for Coronation festivities, but these had to be postponed when the king fell seriously ill from appendicitis. But the king recovered, sport was held in Balaclava Road recreation ground, along with 'ventriloquism, Punch and Judy, marionettes, gramophone records, etc.'. A procession of decorated motorcars and bicycles passed through the streets and 'select dancing' took place in a reserved enclosure.

An appeal was later launched to erect a monument to commemorate the Coronation, led by Dr. Owen Coleman, Chief Medical Officer. Plans for the memorial were received from 116 architects, and the design of Mr. John Johnson for a clock tower were selected. A site was donated on Claremont Road, and donations were made towards the foundations, the clock mechanism, and the bronze plaque of the king and queen. Unfortunately, the remainder of the funds for the memorial were not forthcoming and Dr. Coleman was forced to make a further public appeal in 1907 for the balance of £213. The memorial was finally completed in 1908, just two years before King Edward himself died.

The population of Edwardian Surbiton continued to grow rapidly. By 1910, it had risen to 18,747, most of the increase occurring in Tolworth. The death rate also remained low, maintaining Surbiton's reputation, in the words of Dr. Coleman, making his 32nd annual report, as a 'Salubrious Suburb'. But the low birth rate, noted at the time of the Extension Bill Inquiry, had picked up, as young families moved into the rapidly growing residential areas.

Edwardian Amusements

Surbiton retained its prosperous air through the Edwardian period. The Surbiton Beagles continued their meetings at the Kennels on Acre Hill in Chessington, the Surbiton Choral Society continued to perform at the assembly rooms. A thriving programme of lectures and talks was held at the assembly rooms, such as the 1901 lecture given by the celebrated missionary, Dr. Paton, who spoke about the adventures and narrow escapes of missionaries among cannibals in the New Hebrides. The event attracted a record audience.

Every summer there were fêtes for members of local societies, such as that of Surbiton Hill Working Men's Club which held its fête in a meadow off Ewell Road in 1910, complete with athletic sports and racing. Football was becoming popular at this time and Surbiton Park Football Club was formed in 1899.

Concerts and parties were held at the Gables in aid of the private military hospital set up by the Coopers for casualties from the Boer War. Patients were brought up from the Cape on the Princess of Wales' Hospital Ship. Some may have been suffering from sexually transmitted diseases and were brought to the Gables to be treated by Dr. Cooper.

59   *Patients at the Gables.*

60   The Gables theatre converted into a ward.

On 19 January 1901, a concert was given at the Gables by the choir of the Chapel Royal at Hampton Court. The concert was attended by the Princess of Wales, soon to be Queen Alexandra, who presented each of the hospital patients with a 'souvenir of their soujourn [sic] at the hospital'. The gift included a neat pocket book with a portrait of the princess. Silver cigarette and card cases were also presented to Sir Alfred and Lady Cooper to thank them for their work.

Charitable fêtes and events continued at the Gables long after the hospital had closed and the Coopers had left. A typical event was the performance of a pageant 'The Masque of Time' at the Gables in the summer of 1909, attended by the Duchess of Albany. The pageant, written by Mr. Hugh Mytton of Surbiton Hill, presented a conflict between Spring and Father Time, with the national anthem sung at the end. Proceeds were used to help disabled people in the district.

New Currents

In spite of the concerts and pageants, clear social changes were occurring. The *Surrey Comet* noted in September 1907:

> The solitary fact that there are now within its boundaries 600 tenements of less than five rooms shows how different is the town from the select oasis of suburbia of which St Mark's was the centre, even down to the 80s. Southborough and the parishes of Tolworth and Hook have been added to the original area in recent times and the incursion and administration of these older portions have exercised their influence on the management of the united district.

Edwardian Surbiton seemed a less settled and peaceful place than previously. 1905 was marked by several divorces and an attempted shooting by a local grocer of a money lender. In the same year, Laura Dunnage, an occupant of Avenue Elmers

SURBITON URBAN DISTRICT COUNCIL'S PROPOSED OMNIBUS BILL.
Estimated Cost, about £100,000.

THE PATIENT ASS, OR, THE SURBITON RATEPAYER.

Head Donkey Man : NOW THEN, CHAPS, HURRY UP WITH THAT OMNIBUS ! WE SHALL VERY LIKELY GET IT HITCHED ON BEFORE HE NOTICES IT.

Active Member of the Association for the Prevention of Cruelty to Ratepayers : STOP! STOP! THE POOR BEAST CAN HARDLY CARRY HIS PRESENT LOAD.

who had previously lived in Albury House, wrote to the *Surrey Comet* to comment on the 'recent cruel destruction of the owls in the district ... They were a great pleasure and interest to our whole household'. She added: 'It is certainly very unsafe to fire any kind of gun among a number of small gardens like these'.

The countryside was receding. Housing developments during this period included Beaconsfield Road and Gordon Road, built between 1901 and 1910 on land owned by the Rev. John Jemmett of Albury House. In spite of development, Berrylands Farm continued to maintain a herd of over 100 choice pedigree Jersey, Guernsey and Shorthorn cows, delivering milk locally up until the 1930s. Mrs. Ellen Brown remembered working at Berrylands Dairy, on Ewell Road; the archway to the yard remains opposite the *New Prince* pub. Arriving before 3 o'clock in the morning, she loaded the milk into barrels which she had to push. 'It meant your head going forwards and your legs going backwards to stretch to push the weight of it ... and on the hill, Clay Hill, I used to have to push up that when it was deep clay.'

There is evidence that support was falling to the local churches at this time. Canon Potter, the successor to Archdeacon Burney at St Mark's, spoke in a sermon in 1908 about a fall in the funding for the church schools from seatholders. He spoke of his determination not to cut funding to the schools, and considered raising a mortgage to cover the shortfall.

A Rise in the Rates

Edwardian Surbiton was marked by a steady improvement in the range and quality of local services. However, this was also accompanied by a steady rise in rates, which reached 3s. 5½d. in the pound in 1907, equivalent to a total average

63 Adolf Zimmern, seen here in 1910. His son, Sir Alfred, was the co-founder of the Geneva School of International Studies and educational counsellor to the President of the American International College. Zimmern lived with his father at Oakhill Dene, which used to stand on the site of St Matthew's Primary School playing fields.

payment of 38s. per head, compared with just 4s. at the time of the first Improvement Act.

Some of the increase was attributed to the need to pay off debts accrued since 1895, when the Urban District was constituted. But much of the increase was related to the increased cost and depth of what Richardson described as 'necessary luxuries'.

Expenditure had been raised by 3d. in the pound in 1901 to fund a range of public schemes. These included the purchase from Lord Lovelace of the Balaclava Road and Hook recreation grounds, previously leased, at a cost of £10,000 and £5,500 respectively. A decision was taken at a meeting in February 1902 to rename the Balaclava Road ground after the 'most glorious reign the world has ever known'. Money was later borrowed in 1907 to build a cricket pavilion in the Victoria ground.

Further municipal schemes were promoted by a Private Omnibus Bill, which was presented to Parliament in December 1905. The Bill sought to give Surbiton a range of powers on specific projects

61 Above left. The Surbiton Watercress and Flower Girls Mission. A Christian Mission for vulnerable girls, possibly associated with the Kingston Hill Princess Louise Home. Surrey Comet Pictorial Supplement, 11 March 1905.

62 Left. Patient Ass, or the Surbiton ratepayer. Newspaper cartoon, 1903. A response to the proposed Omnibus Bill, eventually passed in 1905.

64 *Tram passing the Surbiton clock tower and Claremont Road. The tower was completed in 1908 to commemorate the Coronation of King Edward VII.*

such as the power to set up a new riverside wharf, widen certain roads, fix building lines, charge fees for licensing hoardings and to construct a new sewer from Lingfield Avenue, across Surbiton Hill Road and through Maple Road. The Bill also sought the right to extend the previous electric lighting powers, which caused great controversy.

Electric Light

Electricity, according to the *Surbiton Review*, had already been installed at Dr. Cooper's house at South Bank by 1888. Surbiton obtained an electric lighting order in 1891, and in the following year Kingston opened its first power station alongside the Down Hall sewage farms. However, in spite of the order, Surbiton remained cautious, fearful that the cost of providing an electric supply would be too great a burden on the rates.

Nevertheless, the idea was not totally rejected. In the summer of 1900, a survey was held of households in Surbiton who thought they might take electric light. Circulars were sent to 1,420 houses, of which 171 would take the light straight away, giving a total of 10,000 lamps.

Just previous to the the survey, a provisional agreement was made in 1899 between Surbiton Council and the Callenders Cable and Construction Company Ltd. By entering into agreement with a private company, Surbiton Council hoped to reduce the cost and risk to ratepayers to a minimum. Under the agreement, the council would pay the private company to set up and run the power supply for at least five years at previously agreed prices. The company would pay all running and other expenses, even if these were higher than the agreed sum from the council.

The scheme was accepted, and in 1901 Surbiton Council applied to borrow the sum of £50,000 for the new system. Work began on a new power station at the junction of Kingsdowne and Ewell Roads. Meanwhile, Surbiton made an application for authority to extend the electricity supply to Hook, Southborough and Tolworth, areas which were not part of Surbiton when the original Electricity Order was made in 1891. However, this proposal raised an objection from Kingston Gas Company, which feared the increased competition which the new source of power would bring. The

65 *London and Suburban Omnibus Co. bus on Surbiton-Kew Bridge route, outside Kingston Station, 1906.*

66 *Tramway terminus. Outside* Red Lion, *Tolworth,* c.*1910.*

67   *The opening of the Tolworth fountain, opposite the* Royal Oak *pub on Ewell Road, July 1901.*

gas company demanded that Surbiton insert a 'Northumberland Clause' into the agreement, which would prevent Surbiton Council from subsidising the electricity supply from the rates throughout the district. Surbiton responded that any such 'Northumberland Clause' should only apply to the proposed extension to Tolworth and Hook.

The Board of Trade ruled in favour of Surbiton Council, but the gas company refused to give up. On 29 June 1905 the company petitioned the Parliamentary committee of the Board of Trade in the House of Commons; but the Bill was passed as it stood.

The new source of power caught on very quickly. By October 1907 there were 380 consumers, using 80,000 lamps. An application was then made to borrow a further £20,000 for a new boiler, dynamo and buildings at the power station. The loan was secured, but in the following year, there was disagreement between Surbiton Council and Callenders over an alleged unpaid sum of £175 7s. owed by Callenders to the council. A conference was held to resolve the issue. According to Callenders, the unpaid sum was inaccurately calculated, since it came out of their revenue as income tax. At the conference Surbiton Council accused Callenders of charging 'extravagant prices';

68 *Surbiton Drying and Cleaning Works, 12 Maple Road, Surbiton, in the early 20th century.*

69 *W.B. Farmer, butcher, c.1908. The shop used to occupy premises on the west side of Ewell Road close to the junctions of Oak Hill Crescent. The shop is now occupied by a Chinese takeaway, an engraver and a glass and mirror shop.*

70 *J. Lane and Son. Oil, Colour and Glass Merchants. The shop stood at 12 Brighton Terrace, at the corner of Victoria and Brighton Roads. The present building on the site dates from after 1908.*

but Callenders responded by pointing out the increased cost of copper wires and fuse boxes and boards. Surbiton lost the case.

The arrival of electricity in Surbiton made possible new forms of entertainment. The Coronation Picture Theatre opened in the summer of 1911, the year of George V's Coronation with 'Everything High Class and Up to Date'. Previously there had been informal demonstrations of moving pictures at the assembly rooms, such as a screening of 'Our Navy' in January 1901.

The Coming of the Tramways

In April 1905 work began on extending the London and United tramway network to Kingston. A gang of 50 men put up the cables, whilst a further 100 men laid the tracks. Tracks laid from Kingston along Claremont Road divided at the station, with one line passing down Victoria Road, into Brighton Road, to the terminus over the boundary with Long Ditton on Portsmouth Road. The other track went up St Mark's Hill and into Ewell Road, to the terminus near Red Lion Lane in Tolworth.

Some demolitions and road widenings were necessary to lay the tracks. However, the tramways left untouched 'the charming old residence known as Surbiton Hall (formerly known as Surbiton Place), so well beloved by its occupant and so justly admired by everyone who has been privileged to visit it'. To make this possible, trams were diverted into Surbiton Park Crescent, and a shop was demolished at the corner of Surbiton Crescent and Surbiton Road.

By July 1905 great progress had been made, with one track laid up St Mark's Hill and along Ewell Road to Tolworth. At one point, unexpected difficulty was experienced when part of the road was discovered to be laid on ashes. Concrete had to be laid down for the tracks, which were otherwise mounted on wooden blocks.

The network was finally opened to Surbiton on 1 March 1906. The first car left Surbiton Station on the following day at 7.20 a.m. and cars continued their journeys at intervals of five minutes until 9.30 p.m. and then every ten minutes until 11.50 p.m. The first car left Ewell Road at 7.30 a.m. Mr. G.M. Walker, speaking on behalf of the council, joked that the trams would

encourage residents of Kingston to shop in Surbiton 'where they could get just as good value for money'.

The rival bus companies did not intend to let the trams put them out of business. In May 1905 a new motor bus service began between Surbiton Station and Kew Bridge, along the route once followed by the 65 bus. The new buses, each weighing three tons, carried up to 34 passengers, and initially made seven journeys each way every day.

Improvements to the transport system were soon found to have some disadvantages. It was alleged that the noise which the trams were making was emptying properties to either side of the route. At a council meeting in 1909, Dr. Coleman observed that 'to his knowledge, people who were lying ill in houses fronting the tram route had to be removed to other rooms in order to obtain the rest they were entitled to'. In his annual report the following year, Dr. Coleman expressed concern about the dust produced by 'the greatly increased and increasing motor traffic'.

Motor Traffic

By 1910 seven hundred motor vehicles a day were passing along Portsmouth Road. Motor vehicles on the road at this time included Kingston's two motorised fire engines. Surbiton retained a non-motorised engine and Mr. C. Coochey, Chairman of the Surbiton Fire Brigade Committee, noted that should a fire break out in Surbiton, 'it was a hundred to one on Kingston getting there first'.

Road improvements caused the destruction of picturesque features, such as Tolworth pond, at the junction of Kingsdowne Road and Ewell Road. The Kingston Highway Board had considered filling the pond in 1881. When Tolworth fell under the control of Surbiton, the district council claimed ownership of the pond against Lord Egmont, Lord of Tolworth Manor. But the council lost the claim and the pond remained a public watering place for cattle under the manorial rights of the Manor of Tolworth.

In 1897, the pond and surrounding land was bought by Mr. Stephen Kavanagh who lived at Tolworth Lodge Farm. Kavanagh had already

71 *W.A. Ratledge, floral artist, 37 Victoria Road, Surbiton. Photograph taken c.1908. Now site of travel agents.*

72 *Dyson Coal and Coke Merchants, Alpha Road, c.1908.*

73 Claremont Road after a March snow storm.

74 J.E. Allen, draper and milliner, 16 Berrylands Road, Surbiton Hill, c.1908.

75 Electric Parade, Brighton Road, was built in 1904-5 when electricity came to Surbiton. The Black Lion pub, on the left of the picture, was the scene for the public meeting during the Washerwomen Strike of 1872. The clock tower was damaged by a V1 in 1944 and never repaired.

developed much of the land along Ewell Road, and planned to build on the site of the pond as well. However, the people of the area still had ancient manorial rights of access, which had to be protected.

An agreement was eventually reached between Surbiton Council and the developer. Mr. Kavanagh agreed to transfer to the people of Tolworth a plot of land behind the pond, slightly larger than the pond itself. He also agreed to replace the pond by a drinking trough and fountain at a cost of £160.

The Tolworth fountain, with a plaque to Stephen Kavanagh, was ceremonially opened in July 1901. From the Kingston oral archives, Greta Fisk remembered how the day was treated as a Bank Holiday, with a procession of children, a brass band and tea at Tolworth Lodge Farm.

Other Improvements

Drainage problems continued throughout this period. With sewage exceeding the permitted limits, Surbiton was forced to pay towards increased pumping at the Down Hall works. In spite of this, the Thames Conservancy noted that the Surbiton outfall pipe was still overflowing, whilst the need for a proper storm drainage system was also recognised. The Tolworth sewage works was also stretched to capacity. The existing agreement with Kingston would expire in 1912, and the Tolworth works, which had opened in 1891 in Red Lion Lane, were unsuitable for expansion. A new scheme was urgently required.

The council considered a range of new sewage schemes in May 1906. Sites considered for the new works included Lower Marsh Lane, Schwind's Land to the North East of Tolworth and Wood's Land in Malden. Land had already been purchased for the purpose in Malden by the council at a cost of £6,900, with the support of the Local Government Board.

Surbiton Council strongly favoured a scheme which had been proposed by a local engineer, Nicholson Lailey. Under the scheme, new sewage works would be built at a cost of £65,000 on 32 acres of land opposite the Ewell works in Worcester Park. But the scheme was rejected by the Local Government Board in 1907 and the Upper Marsh Lane site was chosen instead.

Surbiton's sewage works opened in 1913, a year after the agreement with Kingston had expired. Kingston amalgamated with the Surbiton system after the formation of the Joint Sewage Board between Kingston, Surbiton, Epsom, Ewell and Malden in 1940.

A Call to Arms

The Surrey Territorial Army was founded on 1 April 1908, formed out of volunteer units which had existed from 1859. In 1909 a recruitment drive was launched and letters were sent out throughout Surbiton. Within three months of the appeal over 950 volunteers had been recruited from the wider district. Surbiton was later the home of the Third Home Counties Field Ambulance Corp and the Royal Army Medical Corp.

Lord Kitchener initially appealed for 100,000 men followed by a further 500,000 in the first few months of the First World War. Surbiton responded to the crisis by setting up an Emergency Committee with Stephen Kavanagh as Chairman. An Austrian 'spy' was arrested at Surbiton Station and later released. At the end of August, a concert was held at Argyle House in aid of the Prince of Wales' National Relief Fund, and a recruitment meeting at St Matthew's Hall in Tolworth was presided over by Canon McNutt. By November recruitment had began for the Kingston Battalion Surrey National Reserve; facilities were also provided for Belgian refugees.

76 *Unveiling of the war memorial in Ewell Road, Surbiton, July 1921. According to the* Surrey Comet, *initial designs for the memorial had to be scaled down when subscriptions failed to achieve the initial target.*

Hastily arranged weddings took place against the backdrop of war. On 7 December 1914, a soldier on short leave from France married his sweetheart, Miss C. Wells Thatcher, at St Mark's Church. The Bridegroom, Lieutenant Leslie Phillips, a signalling officer of the 4th Guards Brigade, appeared at the altar in his war-stained khaki uniform and returned to the Front the following day.

Happily, Leslie Phillips was not killed in battle. Others were not so lucky. Lieutenant Charles Cornish of Lovelace Road, was one of the first Surbiton soldiers to fall, an officer of the Highland Light Infantry. He died at Ypres on 13 November 1914. His name is inscribed on the Menin Gate, along with hundreds of thousands of soldiers whose remains were never found.

At the Armistice, Surbiton was made the discharging centre for the Eastern Command. The surviving soldiers returned to a country and a district profoundly scarred by the sacrifice of the fallen. The Surbiton War Memorial, unveiled in July 1921, records the names of 386 local soldiers who died during the First World War.

CHAPTER
—10—

A PROSPEROUS HAVEN

SURBITON between the wars was not immune from the problems of the age. But national economic and social dislocations left ripples rather than waves on what remained a relatively prosperous area. The growth of new factories powered by electricity, and the availability of cheap land for building protected Surbiton from high rates of unemployment, poverty and labour discontent.

The General Strike of 1926 disrupted rail and bus services, and cut gas lighting. But the *Surrey Comet* bears little evidence of public sympathy towards the strike, which was far from total in the district. On the first day, the earliest train to pass through Surbiton Station, a steam train 'packed as tightly as sardines in a tin,' was 'greeted with cheers'. By the second day, according to the *Surrey Comet*, 'a fairly respectable railway service was maintained ... nearly thirty steam and electric trains making the up journey'. A former London and District Superintendent, Mr. Molyneux, helped out at the station, and a fleet of private motor coaches 'endeavoured to supply the deficiency of the railway service'.

Mrs. Amy Woodgate, with help from the Rev. Martin, set up a depot to which volunteers could enlist to maintain services. By the end of the week, more than 300 'Surbiton Specials'—mostly elderly—had been enlisted. According to the *Surrey Comet*, the team included three unemployed men, with the use of 26 private cars and 14 motorcycles.

Building Boom
The 1920s and 1930s were marked by an unprecedented building boom, both privately and publicly funded. Development was encouraged by the construction of new roads and rail lines.

The Kingston by-pass was the first of its type to be built. The road was opened by the Prime Minister, Stanley Baldwin, on 28 October 1927. Growth in traffic led to the installation of traffic lights in 1934 at the junction with Warren Drive. In 1937 the road was partly widened, and in the same year the Hook Road junction was reconstructed. However, requests made at this time for a subway under the by-pass at Warren Drive were rejected.

The Electric Southern Railway was extended from Motspur Park to Tolworth in May 1938. The line from Tolworth to Chessington South was completed on 28 May 1939, making it one of the last new lines to be built in England this century. The outbreak of the Second World War and post-war Green-Belt legislation meant that the line was never extended to Leatherhead as originally planned.

Surbiton Station was rebuilt between 1936 and 1938 to cope with the increase in the number of travellers; 1,048,981 ordinary and 44,553 season tickets were issued in 1937, compared with 700,477 ordinary and 19,320 season tickets immediately prior to electrification in 1913. The new station, built in modernist style with reinforced concrete, was designed to provide better interchange between fast and slow trains. According to an architectural review of the period, 'the whole is calculated to attract, and is altogether a notable engineering and architectural achievement'.

Council Housing
Surbiton Council first proposed to build public housing shortly after the passing of the 1924 Housing Act. Surbiton proposed to build 50 houses, 25 for the purpose of selling, 25 for letting. Each house was not to cost more than £450 each.

77 *The Hook Bowls Club outing. The photograph was taken outside the South-*borough Arms, c.*1920*.

78 *William Cowley lived at Chessington and was a member of the Surrey Athletics Club. He was also the British Southern and Middlesex track champion.*

79   *Hook Cricket Club, c.1920.*

In 1934, further plans were submitted to build 80 council houses on land adjoining Lower Marsh Lane. The Minister of Health was approached for a loan to build the houses and associated roads and sewers. Two years later, the council gave authority to buy land for 72 houses in Red Lion Lane, and for 115 houses in Clayton Road.

In 1936 the Chief Medical Officer noted that a 'fair percentage' of houses in the Alpha Road area were unfit for human habitation. Most of the houses were 'verminous', and the disrepair of individual houses was 'excessive'. A row of houses in Howard Road was demolished, but the area was not declared a general clearance area as the structure of most of the houses, which were linked to gas and electricity, was sound.

Chalets and Sun Traps

The 1920s and '30s in Surbiton were a boom period for private housing developers. Some flats were built on the sites of old villas, such as the 1930 Surbiton Court in St Andrew's Square and the Wentworth Court development on St Mark's Hill, built in 1937. However most of the new houses were built on green land in Tolworth and Chessington. Houses were built in accordance with new by-laws which provided for sufficient space and light.

The development of Tolworth was a source of pride and excitement. In February 1931 the *Surrey Comet* hailed 'a remarkable achievement, the birth of a township'. By then, the Tolworth Lodge Farm alongside Ewell Road, once the venue for the

80 *Betty Nuthall was born in Surbiton in 1911. She was the first overseas player to win the US women's singles title in 1931.*

81 *St Paul's School, Hook, 1922.*

Surbiton Hounds, had been sold off, the Tolworth Dairy Farm had disappeared, and the toll gate removed close to Broomfield Road. Smith's farmhouse, at the southern end of Alexandra recreation ground, was in ruins. Around this time, Hollyfield Road, remembered by Greta Fisk as a 'lovers lane', was asphalted over, and the water splash over King Charles Road at the end was culverted.

In their place were six-and-a-half miles of streets and 1,333 houses occupied by 6,250 residents. 57 shops had been provided. The district had a new ratepayers' association, and sites had been acquired for a daughter church to St Matthew's, a Roman Catholic church and a congregational church. A tender had already been accepted for a new central school and Tolworth Broadway was planned to by-pass part of Ewell Road.

The *Surrey Comet* praised the new developments. Houses, whilst small, were set in wide and pleasant streets. The whole district was 'light and airy'. As the newspaper noted, 'Tolworth has no slums'.

The 'Egmont Garden City', near to the tramway terminus, was one of the first of the private estates to be completed. In 1926, freehold semi-detached houses were available at the price of £1,075, with four-bedroomed houses slightly more expensive at £1,275. In the same year, Thorne and Co. offered semi-detached houses on Lingfield Avenue at a cost of £895 freehold. Meanwhile, Government Subsidy Houses, built by Thorogoods, were available for sale at £600 in Red Lion Lane.

The Kingston by-pass was not the busy and noisy road which it has become. Housing developments along the by-pass profited from the glamour of the new concrete-surfaced highway.

82   Arthur Pointer's grocery shop, 320 Hook Road, seen here in the 1930s-40s.

Estates development in the 1930s included John Cronk and Son's development on the Hook Rise, offering £595 for freehold houses, £850 for semi-detached. The nearby Oakcroft Estate offered 'Clean Concrete Roads, new shops, splendid school facing Estate'. Houses on sale in the Haycroft Estate towards Hook, named after the large Haycroft House which had previously stood on the site, were available at prices between £895 and £995. Nearby was the Hooklands Estate, developed by L.H. Ransom.

The sale of Berrylands Farm and the opening of Berrylands Station paved the way for the development of an entirely new neighbourhood. Houses became available on Berg's 'Berrylands Estate' in Spring 1934. Using the slogan 'Happiness within', Berg's advertised semi-detached houses from £775 freehold, and detached from £875. Larger houses on Parks Road and Berrylands Road were priced at £1,500 freehold; these offered four large bedrooms, and an oak panelled hall. Houses on

Berrylands Park Estate, centred on Raeburn Avenue, were offered at the slightly cheaper price of £675 freehold.

Away from the by-pass, Wimpey developed the Surbiton Hill Park Estate centred on Grand Avenue in 1934. Advertisements described the neighbourhood as

> renowned for its good class residents ... Beautiful rolling countryside is within strolling distance of these soundly built semi-detached houses. Wimpey have spared no efforts to make these houses some of the finest ever built. Three bedrooms, spacious living rooms, kitchens with every labour saving device and plenty of cupboard room.

The adjoining Surbiton Estate around Elmbridge Avenue was also developed by Wimpey, and the first houses became available in 1936. Potential purchasers were whisked from Berrylands Station 'by private car' to view the new houses, which were said to adjoin 'a large natural park which can never be built on'.

Laura Callaghan was one of many first-time residents of Tolworth. She recalled that larger houses were advertised as 'chalets' while the smaller houses were referred to as 'sun traps'. She remembered that her neighbours

> were inclined only to open the door a little way, unless they had their best clothes on and they were absolutely spick and span, then they invited you into the hall ... they were what people termed as suburban.

A darker current to the new estates was highlighted at Easter 1935, when a tragedy occurred in a new house in Tolworth. A young father strangled his wife and two children before committing suicide by inhaling gas. The victims lay undetected for a week.

New Employment

The rapid construction of reasonably-priced housing was matched by the development of new factories. By 1939, factories along the by-pass included the Mollart Engineering Works, Helena Rubenstein Cosmetics, Parnall Aircraft, Andre Rubber Co. Ltd., Betty Joel Celluloid Printers, Western Electric and Fox & Nicholls. Other small companies in Surbiton at this time included Opticrafts, behind the Plough Garage on Ewell Road, and Colt Heating and Ventilating in Langley Avenue.

Surbiton's Newest Daughter

After Tolworth and Berrylands, developers turned their eyes towards the fields of Chessington, 'newest daughter of the Queen of the Suburbs'. The Local Government Act of 1929 had led to a General Review of County Districts, which recommended the transfer of Chessington from Epsom Rural

83   An advertisement for new housing in Berrylands, May 1934.

84   *Gilders Road, Chessington in the 1930s.*

District to Surbiton. The order was confirmed by the Surrey County Council Order of 1933.

As early as 1921 the *Surrey Comet* had warned readers: 'Those who wish to see the beautiful view from the porch of Chessington Church must not delay as quite recently the builders have begun to blot it out, and their work of disfigurement proceeds rapidly'. At this time, work had already begun on the Copt Gilders housing estate.

In October 1936, the *Surrey Comet* returned to Chessington, to find a mix of town and country:

> Cows grazing between piles of drain pipes and the trenches dug for them, suntrap villas built alongside farm cottages, concrete roads running between haystacks; a shopping centre far from any bus route.

The main Leatherhead Road was lined with posters announcing new housing developments served by concrete roads. These included the Chessington Court Estate built by Chessington Estates Ltd. in the grounds of the old mansion. Houses were available for £520 with two reception

rooms, a kitchenette, bedrooms and a tiled bathroom. But the rapid development of housing was not immediately matched by a provision of essential amenities. Leatherhead Road only received street lighting in 1936. In the same year, 84 houses, the village hall and the new school in Moor Lane area were still without electricity.

Consilio et Animis

The question of Surbiton seeking a borough charter was first discussed by Surbiton Council in November 1932. The issue was again considered in November 1933, and an application was formally made to the Privy Council in the following year.

Speaking at a meeting of the Tolworth rate-payers association in 1935, Mr. S. Hall offered the opinion that when Surbiton became a borough it would attract 'a better type of representative ... the Dignity of a borough council was very attractive'. The proposed charter would reconstitute the council with a mayor and aldermen. There would be 27 members representing nine wards.

Kingston, whose title of Royal Borough had been confirmed in 1927, opposed the scheme. The borough's ambitions towards its southerly neighbour were given voice by Mr. Chuter Ede, later Kingston Alderman and Chairman of Surrey County Council, in a 1933 speech at Kingston Guildhall.

Great as the past has been, it is as nothing to the greatness of the Corporation when it gets its full opportunity of extending local government for the whole of that community which, in spite of the dots on the map, is Kingston.

Kingston, as it had done at the time of the 1894 Extension Bill, again set out its case in an official letter. The letter claimed that a saving of £5,000 could be made by merging the two districts, with economies in the cost of running the sewage works and public library and in providing electricity. Kingston also invited Surbiton to contribute to a new swimming pool in Denmark Road, to be built at a cost of £78,000.

Surbiton responded by claiming in a letter that its sewage works were recognised as being 'thoroughly up to date' while recent extensions

85   An aerial view of Warren Drive, Tolworth, in the 1930s.

86 *An aerial view of Messrs. Thorogood's Haycroft Estate., c.1933.*

would be paid for by the 'increased rateable value of the district'. Motor tractors and trailers collected Surbiton's refuse, while Kingston still used horse-drawn vehicles. Surbiton's wide roads needed few improvements, unlike the old roads of Kingston; a public library in Kingston would be of little use to Surbiton residents. Surbiton also claimed that the cost of electricity would 'be reduced quite independently of amalgamation'. The letter concluded that

> Surbiton was of independent origin and growth, has throughout its history been recognised as a separate unit of government, and has provided its own services and paid for them, and it should not now be called upon either to surrender its independence or be saddled with expenditure from which it will derive no benefit.

An inquiry into Surbiton's application for borough status was held in November 1934, and in June 1935, the Government requested a draft charter and scheme. The charter was approved in May 1936, officially granted on 1 July 1936 and formally handed over by the Lord Lieutenant of Surrey on 16 September 1936. It was one of the few documents signed by King Edward VIII as King.

The new Surbiton coat of arms was granted by the College of Arms. Charred stumps on the shield signified the Burnt Stub House in Chessington. An elm tree recalled the former Elmbridge Hundred, of which Tolworth and Hook were a part. The bridge at the top indicated the railway, to which Surbiton owed its development, with the lion of St Mark's resting on the bridge. The shield was supported by two stags from the Coutts family arms. Surbiton also acquired a motto—*Consilio et Animis*—By wisdom and courage. Civic regalia included a silver cigarette case donated by the residents and ratepayers of Chessington. A silver loving cup was presented by the Wandsworth and District Gas Company.

The Blue Lagoon?
In spite of being one of the lowest rated districts in London, the district council had assured ratepayers that rates would not rise when Surbiton became a borough.

The pledge was not kept. In March 1936 a rise in the rates of one shilling and four pence in the pound was announced and further rises were said to be 'inevitable'. According to the Finance Chairman, Mr. W. Sanger, 'Surbiton was suffering from growing pains and they could not have a district develop so quickly without large initial expense'. He pointed out that the new estates of small houses, with low rateable values made a large demand on borough services such as refuse collection and street lighting.

However, the expense of extra offices for the increased borough staff was also acknowledged to be a factor in the rate rise. Financial difficulties led to the deletion of £1,500 from the budget set aside to celebrate the granting of borough status.

Aside from these factors, a rise in the rates was inevitable given the growing expectation for public amenities during the 1920s and '30s.

Claremont Crescent Gardens had been bought by Surbiton Council in 1935. The council had also bought the Fishponds Estate for £10,000 as a public park; the estate had previously belonged to Charles Butler, the tobacco merchant. In the previous year, the open-air 'Surbiton Lagoon' was completed in Raeburn Avenue, Berrylands.

The naming of the pool caused some controversy. One name considered for the pool was the 'The Blue Lagoon', but this was rejected on the grounds that 'those who had studied the book of that name' might expect 'something in the way of a return to nature'.

The new pool would open every day between 30 April and 30 September. The price was set at 6d. for adults from Monday to Fridays, 3d. for children under 14, 1s. for adults on Saturday morning and 6d. for Saturday afternoon.

Surbiton Lagoon opened unofficially at 6.30 a.m. on Monday 30 April 1934. According to the *Surrey Comet*, a queue of three young men had formed even at that early hour. The official opening took place on 27 June, with a display of high-diving and water polo by members of the Empire Swimming Club, including channel swimmers Miss Ivy Hawke and Mr. E. Temme of Tolworth.

The *Surrey Comet* was enthusiastic about the new pool:

> low red and white buildings with red tiled gabled rooves [have] a summery appearance, even in the weaker sun of spring ... and when one catches a first glimpse of the crystal clear water of the baths moving gently behind the tumbling turbulence of the fountain, it is really a temptation to dive in and swim and splash and laugh with the sheer joy of being alive.

New Schools and Hospitals

Following a public appeal, the new Surbiton Hospital was opened by the Duchess of Gloucester in July 1936. Occupying the former site of Hill House, once the home of William Walter, the hospital was described by the *Surrey Comet* as 'modern in design, equipment and accommodation'. In the same year, new ward blocks were added to the Tolworth Hospital.

87 *Interior of Surbiton station after rebuilding, 1938.*

88   *Tolworth Broadway in the 1930s. The meadow on the right survived until the building of Tolworth Tower.*

In October 1920 a meeting was held to discuss the provision of secondary education. At this time there were no state-funded secondary schools in Surbiton, although Surbiton High School had already arranged to take a number of pupils from elementary schools on scholarships. Surbiton Council also provided some funding for the Tiffin Schools. A decision was later taken to set up a boys' grammar school in Surbiton.

The Chairman of the Board of Governors, Mr. Wilcocks bought Albury House as a location for the new school, formerly the home of Dr. Williams, who had produced 'Pink Pills for Pale People'. The school opened on 16 September 1925, with 69 boys and reached a capacity of 200, divided into four houses: Villiers, Egmont, Coutts and Lovelace. An extension was added in 1935.

Other educational amenities included Tolworth Girls' School which opened in 1932. The Surbiton library first opened in 1929 with 2,500 books and the foundation stone for the present library building was laid on 2 September 1931.

Training for Life

Hillcroft College developed from an experimental institution set up by Ruth Hinder at Cheshunt. This evolved into a new college which first opened at Beckenham in 1920 with 11 students. Sponsors included the YWCA, Reading University College and the Royal Holloway College, as well as commercial and private donations.

Phoebe Walter, Secretary to the YWCA Education Committee, oulined the role of the college in a magazine article in 1919:

What will the students be trained for? Surely the answer to this is 'for life'. There need be no talk of 'rising' from one social sphere to another, or of climbing the 'ladder' of education. Education is not a ladder but a highway, where all free citizens have the right to walk.

The college at Beckenham proved to be too small and in 1925 Wilberforce Bryant's former house at South Bank was purchased. Alongside teacher training, the college offered courses in many other subjects, including short courses for unemployed women during the Depression.

New Churches
Work began on the new congregational church in Tolworth in autumn 1933, £3,900 having been raised out of the total cost of £5,000. The new building was completed in February 1934. The *Surrey Comet* praised the 'simple dignity' of the new church, with its 'straight lines and angles'.

The new St George's Church in Hamilton Avenue, Tolworth, was consecrated in June 1934 as a daughter church to St Matthew's. Built for just £5,354, the building comprised an area for services and a meeting hall divided by a roller shutter. At the dedication, the new vicar, the Rev. Thornton, informed his parishioners:

> Our part of Tolworth includes 1,750 new houses ... They already have shops and cinema and will shortly have a public house. When we have provided a church, it will ... become a rallying point for the forces of Christ in their midst.

In 1923 St Andrew's made a bid to break away from the parish of St Mark's and form its own parish. The church pointed to the rapid rise in the parish population, which was close to the 4,000 required for independence. By becoming independent, the church would be eligible to receive a grant of £250 per annum to pay the stipend of an assistant priest. St Andrew's eventually became a separate parish in 1933.

In spite of active church building, there were signs of a decline in church attendance and in 1934 the superintendent of St Mark's Children's Church noted that attendance was 'not as good as it used to be'.

Chessington Airport
In 1934, a proposal to build a Municipal Aerodrome was made by representatives of Surbiton, Esher, Malden and Coombe and Kingston Borough Councils. The favoured site for the new airport was Byhurst Farm between Chessington and Malden Rushett, which would be served by an extension of the Southern Railway.

The proposals were discussed at a 'stormy' public meeting at the assembly rooms in June. Speaking for the Air Ministry, Mr. Ivor McClure expressed the opinion that the Chessington site was the 'only one practicable for use as an aerodrome out of eight sites which he had inspected in Surrey', but he pointed out that the site needed 'a great deal of levelling, the cost of which might be prohibitive'. Nevertheless, he insisted there were 'insufficient aerodromes next to London'. An opposing view was put forward by Mr. D. Wilkes, who remarked that 'aviation was a means of luxury travel for the wealthy and not for the masses'. He claimed that there were already 19 municipal aerodromes in the country which were being run at a loss.

According to the *Surrey Comet*, the proponents of the scheme were met with 'shouts, interruptions and derisive laughter'. The audience at the meeting voted overwhelmingly to reject the proposal, which was later also rejected by Surbiton Borough Council. As the *Surrey Comet* commented, it was very hard to say whether the proposal would have been a 'monument of folly or of wisdom'. The name Chessington never appeared on civilian airport schedules, although a site in Mansfield Road was later used by the RAF.

Should Women Be Banned?
In September 1934, Surbiton Council held a debate on the question of whether women should be banned from certain types of jobs as council employees. At that time, there were 15 women on the council staff, but a recommendation to promote one female member of staff prompted a council debate.

Mr. Sanger noted that the experience of the civil service was that 'women could take executive and administrative appointments'. He would support a resolution for the total exclusion of women, 'but having admitted them, to give them no chance, however efficient, was wrong'.

Mr. Southwell took the opposite view and moved an amendment that women should only be employed as typists and junior clerks. In his view,

> with all respect to women in business, a man looked for work so that he could reach a position and marry and have a home and children. A woman looked for work as a stop gap from the time she left school until some man could marry her.

When this amendment was defeated, Mr. Bailey proposed that no women at all should be employed by the council.

But Surbiton Council voted against sexual prejudice and passed the resolution that all clerical appointments, junior and non-junior, should be advertised, with sex being no bar to the appointment or subsequent promotion.

I'm No Angel

Surbiton's spirit, as reflected in local newspapers, was optimistic during the 1930s. Leisure time was increasing and opportunities for recreation and new forms of popular entertainment were more freely available.

Occasions for celebration were provided by the granting of the Borough Charter in 1936 and the Silver Jubilee, when new commemorative gates were built at Surbiton Hospital. The 1937 Coronation was celebrated with a firework display. Open-air services were held at the Alexandra and King Edward recreation grounds and the 'Ace of Spades' held a Coronation Ball.

The 'Ace of Spades' on the Kingston by-pass was one of the smartest road houses in the south-east. Opened in 1927 on a rural site and alongside a new fast road, it became fashionable during the late 1920s and early '30s and was said to have been visited by members of the royal family. A payment of 3s. on Saturdays gave access to the ballroom, which opened in 1934. Guests could dance to Percy Chandler's Band, enjoy cabaret, or swim 'in crystal clear water, perfectly sterilised without chlorine and warmed to 75 degrees'. The pool and adjoining sun beach were 'open all day and night' and 'full restaurant service' was provided at the pool side. The swimming pool was destroyed when the Hook underpass was built in 1958.

Surbiton gained two new cinemas in 1934. The Tolworth Odeon was opened by Sir George Penny MP on 9 January, one of 17 similar cinemas being built around London at that time. With 'up to date heating and ventilation' the 1,000-seat cinema was decorated in a colour scheme of pink, mauve, blue, silver and Chinese red. At the first screening, Eddie Cantor and the 76 Gorgeous Goldwyn Girls' appeared in *The Kid from Spain* along with Laurel and Hardy in *Twice Two*, a Mickey Mouse cartoon and the Gaumont British News.

Surbiton Odeon opened a few months later. The ceremony on 14 April was attended by Anne Grey, a 'celebrated stage and screen star born in Surbiton'. The cinema was designed by Surbiton architect Joseph Hill. According to the *Surrey Comet*, the 'sheer wall faces', 'simple fenestration' and 'bold motif of … massive pylons' illustrated 'contemporary architecture in all its simplicity and dignity'. A few weeks after opening, the cinema screened *I'm no Angel* starring Mae West.

In 1931 Mr. R Goddard, a slate merchant, bought Burnt Stub as a site for a private zoo. The zoo first opened to the public in July and welcomed 2,100 visitors on August Bank Holiday. Chessington soon became the largest private zoo in the country. For an adult admission of 1s. 3d., visitors in 1934 could see 'the finest lions in captivity' along with leopard cubs, kangaroos and chimpanzees. The zoo also offered a daily 'All Animal Circus'. Visitors were assured that animals were trained 'with patience and without cruelty'. Dancing in the licensed restaurant was held every Saturday night from 7.30 till midnight. Advertising played freely on the historical associations of the site, both real and fictitious; 'Charred oak-beams', dating allegedly from the Civil War, were displayed in the ballroom.

Celebrities of the time with Surbiton connections included Phyllis Dixey—'The Girl the Lord Chancellor Banned'—who grew up in Surbiton. Her show 'Peek a Boo' with husband, Jack Tracey, was followed by wartime appearances in shows of statuesque nudity at the Windmill Theatre. Enid Blyton lived for a time with a family on Hook Road, and Alfred Bestall, who drew Rupert Bear in the *Daily Express* for 30 years, lived at Cranes Park from 1935.

CHAPTER

11

SURBITON'S WAR

SURBITON'S War began with the wail of air-raid sirens during morning service. About half the congregation at St Matthew's Church got up to leave, but were turned back by the ARP warden to scenes of general confusion and mild panic.

The borough had played its part in the war-effort long before then. In 1937 plans were submitted to build a Royal Air Force base at Hook, and by 1938 the RAF station was under construction. Barracks were built to the south of Mansfield Road, and a concrete anchor for barrage balloons was also built. This later became a barrage balloon training centre.

Detailed plans had been made for civil defence well before the outbreak of war. Regular training sessions were conducted throughout 1939, including a simulated raid on the night of 11 June which involved 87 separate incidents. The borough was divided into 40 ARP districts, each with its own brick and concrete ARP post, and communal shelters were dug at many sites, including Claremont Gardens, St Andrews's Square, the grounds of Hillcroft College, Warren Drive, Berrylands Road, the Lagoon pool and the *Toby Jug* pub on the Kingston by-pass.

By 27 December 1939, over 1,400 wardens had been appointed, of whom 425 were paid either as full- or part-time workers. Payment of wardens was at the discretion of the borough council, which had expected that a greater percentage would work voluntarily; the mayor, Councillor E.B. Ames, was 'left wondering that certain people were taking wages for their work'.

Other wartime preparations included the provision of 96 acres for allotments along the Hogsmill, between Raeburn and Grand Avenues, parallel with Alexandra Drive and along Tolworth stream. Land was also requisitioned for allotments at the Fishponds. In total, 1,224 plots were provided.

Open conflict soon flared up between the wardens of posts B11 and B12 in Berrylands Ward and representatives of the borough council. The two district wardens of these posts had refused to man the new shelters continuously, arguing that there was no reason why they should not remain on duty in their private houses until the siren sounded, when they could transfer in seconds to the ARP posts. In the words of one of the district wardens:

> Conditions [in the Posts] do not permit of their being manned 168 hours per week by unpaid wardens being on duty for eight or more hours at a stretch, whilst such volunteer helpers as these could work in a private house during the day and in the event of a raid be available in the brick post within 60 seconds.

The two rebel wardens were quickly dismissed from their duties and two full-time paid wardens were appointed in their place. However, this did nothing to resolve the situation. On 8 November, 535 wardens at the two posts came out in support of the district wardens. A deputation asked to speak to the mayor, but their request was turned down. The wardens of post B12 responded by walking out *en masse*. One of the wardens explained:

> All of us have resigned with considerable regret, especially as in many cases we have done nearly two years voluntary service and many of us did not care two hoots whether we had to man one of the newly built brick posts or a warden's house, using the post merely as an action centre in case of a raid. It would have meant a share of the cost of a telephone extension and the light and heating of a room and of one warden ... but it would have saved the nation well over £300 a year'.

89 *Rev. Featherstone and the choir of St Paul's, Hook, 1942.*

90   *St Mark's Church, ruined after the Blitz.*

The issue had still not been resolved by 10 January, when the borough council received a report on the situation. Councillor Mear pointed out that

> ... disaffection was only at two of the five posts in Berrylands Ward and the numbers affected were a very small minority. It was all because a few wardens considered that they were in a better position to run their posts according to their own ideas rather than as they had been instructed by the government.

One of the district wardens responded by publishing a letter in the *Surrey Comet* critical of the way in which the conflict had been handled. He commented:

> Two of the wardens who had been dismissed have very fine war records. One of them served with the Forces both in the South African war and the Great War, whilst the other won his commission in France where he was awarded the MC for an act of gallantry when in charge of his tank. I should say at least fifty percent of the other wardens saw service with HM forces in 1914-1918.

The mayor regarded the attitude of the wardens as a personal insult. 'I know of no Mayor who would tolerate being insulted in such a way, and I shall attempt to do nothing more for the "rebels".' The dismissed wardens were not reinstated and the other wardens returned to their posts.

Before the Blitz

The early months of 1940 were a time of quiet consolidation. Councillor Mrs. Woodgate of the Surbiton WVS issued an appeal in the *Surrey Comet* of 27 January 1940: 'No woman in Surbiton, whatever her age or ability, need be without work of some national importance which she can do in her spare time'. With meat from the butchers difficult to obtain, a rabbit club was established in Tolworth and plans were put in motion to provide 42 extra beds at Surbiton Hospital as part of the National Emergency Scheme under the Ministry of Health. The maternity section was closed, and 70 beds were made ready for war casualties alongside 36 beds for normal civic needs. Provision was also made to receive refugees fleeing from occupied Belgium, Holland and France: 13 houses were requisitioned for refugees on 16 May 1940, with 53 available by October. Demonstrations of wartime cookery took place at 'Cranhurst' on Surbiton Hill Road and arrangements were made for doctors to man each of the first-aid posts in the borough.

The First Raids

Civil defence arrangements were put to the test on the night of the 26 August when the district received its first direct hits from German bombers; minor damage was caused to a line of 14 houses just south of the *Fox and Hounds* pub on Leatherhead Road. A local ARP warden described the German planes appearing during the first raids:

> like a flock of birds. Then two lots of our planes appeared, one on either side, and began to close in on the Germans. They immediately began to disperse, and then the jettisoning of their bombs began, and so did dog fights between our planes and theirs.

The bombers returned on the night of 9 September. Considerable damage was caused in Elmbridge Avenue, where Surbiton's first civilian

91 *Surbiton ARP districts. The black dots mark ARP posts.*

92   The British Restaurant in the Parish Hall, Hook.

fatality suffocated in the wreckage of her house. On the same night, a plane carrying three German pilots crashed into the Maori Sports Ground; the pilot and crewmen were killed on impact, there bodies taken to Surbiton Hospital.

Bombing raids continued throughout the month; on 29 September, Ravenscar Road and Largewood Avenue received several hits, causing further fatalities. Then on the night of 2 October, St Mark's Church was almost totally destroyed by an oil bomb. Due to censorship restrictions, the incident was not reported until December. Although air-raid wardens had arrived quickly on the scene, fire had already engulfed the building and attempts to put out the blaze were hampered by a shortage of water in the mains. During the same night, three people died at Chessington Zoo when the public shelter received a direct hit.

Public shelters soon became overcrowded, partly because they were being used as dormitories in spite of the availability of several thousand Anderson shelters. The *Surrey Comet* reported that over 150 people regularly sought refuge in the shelter at the Surbiton Lagoon, though it had only been built to accommodate 70 people. To cope with the demand, extra brick shelters were built at Cottage Grove and in the grounds of Croylands on Upper Brighton Road, at an estimated cost of £310 and £300 respectively.

Raids continued until Christmas and beyond. On 27 December 1940, a high explosive bomb caused devastation and several deaths in Villiers Close, with a further fatality in Addison Avenue on New Year's Eve.

Salute the Soldier

In January 1941, Surbiton joined forces with Kingston and Malden in 'War Weapons Week', with the aim of providing £350,000 in war bonds and other loans towards the cost of a destroyer. In support, Sir Neville Henderson, British Ambassador to Berlin at the outbreak of war, spoke at the Odeon Cinema and a captured German plane was put on show in Tolworth Broadway. School concerts and whist drives were organised. The appeal quickly exceeded the £300,000 mark, with £327,000 raised by the end of the week, including £2,270 19s. 9d. donated by Surbiton schools.

Though less frequent, raids continued well into 1941. Tolworth was particularly badly hit, with two fatalities occurring in Ravenscar Road in March. Six people were killed in Douglas Road on 28 July 1941 and the bombs returned to the same road the following month, causing a further fatality. Doreen Conroy, a child during the war, recalls the bomb site at the corner of Douglas and Ewell Roads:

> There was a toy shop and a dairy and it was flattened ... there were some people that were on that bomb site cutting up huge pieces of shell, ... I remember the oxyacetylene welder torches they used and their goggles and these big sheets of steel they used to cut through ... and cart it back on a trolley.

In January the Borough Medical Officer had commented on the 'appalling' conditions in many of the public shelters. In addition, 400 small Anderson shelters in the borough were said to be flooded, with 1,850 other cases of unsatisfactory conditions. In response, 3,855 new Morrison shelters were laid on free of charge, and those who could afford to pay bought a further 1,286. The number of full-time wardens was increased from 89 to 109 and 41 mats were provided for the ARP posts. British Restaurants, subsidised by rate-payers, were established at the Co-operative Hall, Tolworth and Hook Parish Hall. This expenditure contributed to the rise in the council rate by 4d. in the new financial year, 1941.

Between 1941 and 1944, three further fund-raising drives were organised by Surbiton Borough Council independently of Kingston or Malden. 'Warships Week' in November 1941 raised £556,000. Sights were raised even higher with a target of £350,000 for the 'Wings for Victory' week of July 1943. This opened with a grand procession from Victoria Avenue to Alexandra recreation ground. Other events included a rabbit

93 *'Salute the Soldier', an advertisement in the* Surrey Comet, *6 May 1944.*

show, a series of variety concerts and displays by the Home Guard and the National Fire Service. The final total of £715,786, more than double the target, exceeded the sum raised by Kingston. But the last fund-raising drive was the most successful: Surbiton's 'Salute the Soldier Week' of May 1944 raised a grand total of £820,000.

Surbiton's factories made a significant contribution to the war effort. The Mollart Engineering Factory, which had developed from a room 50ft. square to a large factory on the Kingston by-pass, pioneered women's rôle in producing high-quality precision electronic components for military purposes. Volunteers also contributed towards the war effort. Mrs. Sydney Gampell turned the lounge of her home into a workshop, where a team of 40 women, mostly housewives, produced components for aircraft in 'remarkable quantities'.

Doodlebugs

As the war turned in the Allies' favour, Surbiton looked to the peace.

Alderman C.H. Bridge had succeeded Alderman Ames as mayor in November 1941 and was re-elected the following year. Bridge lived in Chessington and had a particular interest in developing the area for housing after the war. Under his direction the council put forward plans for the construction of 250 houses between Clayton Road and Mansfield Road in Chessington. The Surbiton Labour Party also put forward their own housing proposals, sponsoring an exhibition in June 1944 about new types of prefabricated housing at Harley Motors showroom.

Extra housing was shortly to become a pressing need. Incendiary raids over the borough intensified in February 1944; hundreds of incendiaries fell over Surbiton during the night of the 23rd,

94 *VE celebrations at Gladstone Road. Arthur Frend, who attended the party as a child, remembers stringing an electrical lead from his house to provide light along the street.*

although many fortunately failed to ignite and only 36 fires were caused.

The sudden onset of V1 raids forced Surbiton to relive the worst terrors of the Blitz. Early in the morning on 12 June, V1 flying bombs fell at two sites in the borough. Twelve people were killed and a further 33 injured—some severely, when a V1 landed on Tolworth Park Road. A husband and wife were also killed at Whitehall Crescent.

Doodlebug raids continued relentlessly during the following weeks. There were deaths at the junction of Portsmouth and Uxbridge Road, in Elmbridge Avenue and at the Royal Eye Hospital on Upper Brighton Road.

Under censorship restrictions, the raids were not reported at all until 21 June. Even then, reports in the *Surrey Comet* dwelt on harmless incidents, such as the explosion of a V1 at the 'singularly appropriate' resting place of Surbiton sewage works. A V1 landing on Chessington Zoo fell

> ... only 20 yards from the cage of the polar bear ... although the bear's temper was soured for a day or two and the animal went off its food and was obviously bruised, complete recovery took place in a fortnight. Burnt Stub was damaged, but the nearest to a human casualty was a man who lost his trousers.

The reality was much grimmer. Oral archives suggest that the most tragic incident of the war in Surbiton occurred as children were being evacuated to Blackpool and Nottingham in mid-July. Dorothy Wright worked with the nursing service and remembered the incident.

> In Tolworth, on that corner ... opposite the skyscraper ... was a big nursery ... we had all these children putting bands on their hands, they were being evacuated to safer places in the country, and that got a direct hit, and there were over a hundred children killed ... It made me ill for a long time. That's the one incident that I do remember very vividly.

Dorothy Wright described how the Green Line buses which were assembled to take the children to the country were used instead as ambulances. Yet the shocking incident remained an official blank, and was not recorded in any local civil defence documents.

Censorship of the V1 raids was partially lifted on 9 September, when the first reliable reports emerged in the *Surrey Comet*. But the raids continued. Two people were killed in Derby Road on 5 October and an ARP warden and his wife died at their house in Ashcombe Avenue on 15 November. Fortunately this was to be the last civilian casualty in Surbiton.

In all, the 22 V1 raids on Surbiton had left 7,422 houses damaged, of which 483 were damaged seriously. During the war as a whole, in 426 incidents, 10,674 houses were damaged, of which 78 had to be demolished. There were 1,704 separate air-raid warnings. Fifty-three civilian deaths were reported, but this figure did not include the Tolworth nursery raid; the real figure was probably much higher.

The End of the War

As 1944 ended, the public mood lifted. Censorship restrictions eased and the *Surrey Comet* was able to report on the individual bravery of Surbiton residents, such as the Picknett family who shared a CBE, a DFC and Pilot Wings between a husband and two sons; the husband had been involved in the planning of the D-Day landings. Tribute was paid to the Civil Defence Services and the local Red Cross and WVS.

Surbiton was fortunate to avoid being hit by V2 rockets, one of which fell on Kingston in early 1945. Planning for peacetime continued; in February, the mayor launched a new appeal, this time for £50,000, to develop Surbiton Hospital. Reports in the *Surrey Comet* reflected a mood of subdued optimism for the future; at the annual meeting of the Surbiton legion on 5 March, Colonel Drayson, who remembered the First World War, expressed the hope that 'we bring our sons to something better'. With the lifting of restrictions, the newspaper was able to report on the contribution made to the war effort by local munitions industries. Plans were made to employ Italian prisoners-of-war held at a camp on Cox Lane at the Surbiton sewage works after the war had ended.

Plans for VE Day included religious services at the Alexandra Road recreation ground and Chessington Church Fields recreation ground, followed by community singing and dancing. The miniature railway at Alexandra Road recreation ground would be set up for rides and entertainments for children were planned. Enquiries were made into the borough's existing stock of bunting.

In the event, VE celebrations got off to what the *Surrey Comet* termed a 'quiet start'. The real festivities began on the following day; 4,000 children attended concerts at the Odeon cinemas and a pig roast was held at the *Toby Jug* pub. Many street parties were held throughout the borough, including Haycroft Road, Norton Avenue, Cranbourne Avenue and Ruxley Lane, Chessington, where an effigy of Hitler was burnt. The mayor arrived unexpectedly at a street party at Northcote Avenue; his car was initially stopped by the street policeman. Later in the week, 60 children were entertained at Greenfield Avenue and the young Petula Clark sang at Bolton Close on the 12th. But fatigue and exhaustion underlay rejoicing; uncertainty remained about the course of the war in Japan, and most of the fighting men were still overseas.

Reconstruction

Alderman A.G. Leach, elected mayor for a second term in November 1944, made the development of the hospital and resettlement schemes his priority. A fund to help returning servicemen was given the target of £2,000.

The end of the war made it urgently necessary to provide affordable private housing and council houses for rent. Some housing schemes had been interrupted when the war began. These included the Barwell Court and Whitehall Park Estates, proposed in the spring of 1939.

At this time, concern was being expressed at the poor progress which the borough council had made in undertaking house repairs. By 17 November 1944, only 377 houses out of 6,500 had been mended. This was a poor record compared with other local authorities in the London area, who registered rebuilding rates of 20 to 25 per cent.

As the war reached its end, new plans called for the construction of houses at Mansfield Road, Chessington and further development at Gosbury Hill. The new houses would occupy the site of old Gosbury Hall, with its observatory and gypsy camping site.

A more ambitious plan proposed by the Surrey Federation of Labour parties envisaged 'clearance of the north east area' of Surrey, with a mass transfer of the population, including half the population of Surbiton, to garden cities in the countryside. 'There must be no suburbia' the plan proclaimed.

The housing programme was soon mired in controversy. The scheme to build council houses at Clayton Road was opposed by the private developers who had received permission to develop the site in 1939. The issue was discussed at a public enquiry in November 1944. But the borough policy was summed up by Councillor Reynolds: 'We desire to build houses to let to the poorer paid workers in the district who cannot buy their own houses ... A private builder who builds houses to let would let a house got to the first person who applied for it'.

Forty-six houses and a primary school were eventually built at Gosbury Hill between 1948 and 1949, following a housing purchase order. Seventy-two flats were also built on the Mansfield Estate. Council houses were also developed on the former site of Chessington Court, which was finally demolished following a compulsory purchase order in 1946.

Private housing schemes also caused controversy. With the end of the war, Ransom and Luck and the Chessington Development Company revived a pre-war application to build houses between Garrison Lane and the Bonesgate Stream. A Public Inquiry in 1938 had approved the scheme, subject to an agreement to transfer some of the land to the borough as open space.

Post-war planning legislation put new obstacles in the way of the scheme. The land was scheduled for inclusion in the proposed Green Belt, whilst the Abercrombie Road Plan had earmarked the site for the D London Ring Road. Planning permission for the development was withdrawn by Surbiton Council, and confirmed in a public inquiry held in 1946, despite a subsequent appeal.

CHAPTER
12

PLANNING THE FUTURE

BY 1951, the population of Surbiton had reached 60,675, roughly double what it had been in 1931. In the same period, the population of Kingston had hardly changed.

Borough Surveyor and Engineer, Mr E. Thirlway, speaking in 1950, estimated that a further 1,236 dwellings houses would be needed by 1955, when the population was expected to have reached 74,000. But Green-Belt legislation prevented development on open land to the south. New development would have to take place in the older areas, and planning decisions taken at this time led to the destruction of many of the patrician villas of Surbiton which had come through the war.

At the time, few objections were raised. The Mayor of Surbiton, Alderman Healey, expressed the view in May 1956 that the council 'was moving away from the idea of Surbiton as Queen of the Surburbs ... most of the large houses would be replaced by high-density development'. There were even calls made in 1963 for the demolition of the King Edward memorial clock to avoid restoration costs. But Alderman Edwards argued that the clock should be repaired, though he added that he 'would not mind at all if all the Victorian houses were pulled down'. A majority of the Council shared his view, and £328 was raised towards the cost of repairs.

One of the first of the old villas to be knocked down was Devonshire House, just outside Surbiton on Ditton Hill, which was redeveloped for houses in May 1954. In the same year Bellaria Park flats opened on a bomb-damaged site between Uxbridge and Palace Roads, offering highly competitive 999 year leases. Dolphin and Ferguson Courts were approved in 1956 and 20 maisonettes with 16 garages were approved at Park Court in 1959.

Development continued during the early 1960s. Exeter and Hove Courts were built in Maple Road during the early '60s. By 1964 there were over 35 blocks of private flats within a one-mile radius of Hollyfield School. But not all planning applications were successful. A planning inquiry was held in March 1962 over proposals to build 21 terraced houses on the site of large villas between 19 and 29 Corkran Road. The developers claimed that the large houses belonged 'to a past era' but the application was quashed though detached houses were later built on the site.

The building of council houses also continued. The Fullers Way Estate was under construction by 1952 and later in the decade 400 homes were built in the grounds of Chessington Hall, which remained standing for a time as a venue for meetings of local groups such as the British Legion. In 1955 the *Surrey Comet* reported on the new estate, with its 'pale walls' and 'delicate green' balconies, which were said to have a 'continental effect'. Interior rooms were decorated in pastel colours. The newspaper contrasted the space and light of the new estate with the privately-rented rooms which many families had previously occupied: 'For the children in particular, it is a healthy life'. Rents were inexpensive; between £1 15s. 3d. to £2 0s. 1d. for a three-bedroomed house, £1 14s. for a flat, and £1 10s. for maisonettes. The residents' only complaint was said to be the lack of shops and unmade roads.

In 1963 the council decided to place a compulsory purchase order on 70 houses in Alpha and James' Road to build new council homes. The houses were among the oldest in the borough, and some had been recently improved by their owners. But the purchase went ahead in spite of opposition

95   The seal pool at Chessington Zoo. Postwar.

and by 1964 Surbiton Borough held a total stock of 1,474 housing units, though some were in Frimley and Camberley.

Social Welfare

Surbiton and Tolworth Hospitals were transferred to the National Health scheme in 1948 and new NHS offices were built on cleared bomb sites on Ewell Road in 1952. Welfare centres were established at Gosbury Hill and in South Place close to Ewell Road. A day nursery was also set up at Fairmead in Tolworth and community centres were established in Hook and Chessington.

New schools continued to be built. These included the Fleetwood Secondary School which opened as an all-boys school in Garrison Lane in March 1954 when the previously mixed Moor Lane School became a girls' secondary school. Ellingham County Primary School opened in July 1955.

Surbiton Grammar School announced in 1960 that it was moving to a new site at Manor Farm in Thames Ditton. According to the *Surrey Comet*, the new site would be 'closer to the area mainly served by the school'. The move made it possible to provide a more suitable site for the Hollyfield Secondary School, which took over Albury House in 1966. In 1963 Christ Church Primary moved to a new site in Pine Gardens and a new extension to Surbiton library opened in 1964.

An Alcoholic's Nightmare

The late 1950s and early '60s saw several controversial planning decisions in Surbiton. These included the decision to build the Tolworth tower on the Kingston by-pass.

The original scheme called for three blocks on the site of the former Tolworth Odeon; this was modified to just two blocks in 1961. The proposed tower, designed by Richard Seifert who went on to build Centre Point, was described by Councillor Cutmore as 'an alcoholic's nightmare' at a council meeting in January 1961.

The plan was opposed by Surrey County Council, but the modified scheme was finally accepted in January 1962 and the building was completed in November 1964. With 22 storeys, and a car park for 615 cars, the tower was the tallest in the Home Counties, and the Fine Fare supermarket on the ground floor was one of the largest in Britain.

In the early 1960s, *The Southampton Hotel* was replaced by the uncompromising Winthrop House alongside Surbiton Station, now itself demolished. Draft plans for the area put forward in November 1964 called for further comprehensive redevelopment of the area, including four new car parks. Victoria Road would be pedestrianised and a new relief road cut through streets to the north, feeding into Cottage Grove. The scheme, if carried out, would have destroyed much of the remaining Victorian core of Surbiton.

Surbiton at this time remained an important manufacturing centre. In January 1961 the new Solartron Electronics Factory opened at Cox Lane in Chessington and in the same year the Crystal Projects Gala Cosmetic Factory was extended. Other major employers in the area included the submarine engineers, Siebe Gorman in Tolworth, the Directorate of Overseas Surveys, and the Animal Health Division of the Department of Agriculture.

A foundation stone for the new St Andrew's Church Hall was laid in 1954. In the following year, the vicar of St Matthew's, Rev. K. Chamberlain, launched an appeal to complete St George's Church in Tolworth. An appeal was launched in 1956 by the Rev. Blair Fish to raise funds to rebuild St Mark's Church. A start was made in March with repairs to the vicarage and the new church was completed in 1960.

Our Lady Immaculate Church was opened at Tolworth in March 1958, £42,000 having been raised in the district towards the total cost of £60,000. In 1964, planning permission was given for a new Roman Catholic church at the corner of Maple Road and Grove Road, though the church was never built.

A large house in the Oak Hill area was the centre for a time of a spiritualist group based around the medium Katherine Hayward and the writer, Liebie Pugh. A chapel and shrine in the house were open to the public, and the group published a book of prophecies, *News from the White House*.

The By-pass

The Kingston by-pass saw continuous improvement during the 1950s and '60s. This was prompted by a major increase in traffic and a shocking series of accidents—between 1950 and 1953, there were four fatal and several serious accidents on the by-pass and 1955 saw five fatal accidents in just a few weeks.

Surbiton Council pressed for lighting, a fence down the middle to deter pedestrians from trying to cross and a speed limit. In particular, a subway was urgently needed on Hook Rise at the Cranbourne Avenue junction, where many accidents involving pedestrians had taken place.

96 *An open-topped horse bus at Chessington Zoo, Burnt Stub, c.1940.*

97 *Andre Rubber Factory. Tolworth Industrial Estate, 1958.*

98 *The Gala Factory, Kingston by-pass, c.1958.*

99 *The Tolworth Odeon before demolition, looking east along the by-pass in the 1950s.*

100 *Kingston Road, Tolworth, in the early 1960s, showing the new Tolworth tower.*

101 *Claremont Road in the early 1960s.*

102   *Tolworth Broadway in the early 1960s.*

103   Victoria Road; the present-day site of Sainsbury's is on the right.

Work on the subway was finally authorised in August 1955 by J. Boyd-Carpenter, MP for Kingston and Minister for Transport. The work was completed in the following year. Arrangements were also made to light the road, although Surbiton Council questioned why it should be made to bear half the cost of electricity.

An underpass at The Ace of Spades had been proposed in 1938, but the idea was shelved when the Abercrombie Plan envisaged a new motorway to the south of the Kingston by-pass, restoring the road to the status of a local feeder road. But this scheme faced considerable opposition; in the meantime the situation on the by-pass grew worse. In 1956, a new plan was put forward to build an underpass at Hook. But this was opposed by a local pressure group, the Kingston By-Pass Association, which proposed instead a scheme designed by Otway for a roundabout and subway on the site. An advantage of this plan was that fewer buildings would need to be demolished at the junction. But these proposals were rejected at an inquiry in July 1956, and work on the Hook underpass began in 1958.

Similar controversy greeted plans in 1964 to build an underpass at the *Toby Jug* roundabout. The scheme entailed the demolition of a garage, By-Pass Motors, whilst 25 houses on Hook Rise North would lose part of their front gardens for a new slip road. Objections were once again overruled and the underpass went ahead.

In spite of the growth of traffic pollution, Surbiton's trolley buses were replaced by Routemaster Diesels in 1961.

Supercilious Surbiton?

In an article from February 1962 in the *Surrey Comet*, Mrs. Phyllis Hayes expressed the opinion that 'living in Surbiton was like living at the top of the mountain'. The image of Surbiton as an unwelcome, unfriendly place—summed up in the tag 'Supercilious Surbiton'—was one which the mayor, Mrs. Betty Greenwood, expressed determination to counter.

Surbiton was not without community spirit. At the Coronation of Queen Elizabeth a dozen street parties were held and 400 children from the Gosbury Hill Estate were entertained at Moor Lane School. 6,280 Coronation mugs were distributed to children, along with 3,406 copies of a commemorative souvenir written by Richard Dimbleby, 'Elizabeth Our Queen'. The Rotary Club organised a party for 300 old people who watched the Coronation on a television screen set up at the assembly rooms; sets were also set up at Moor Lane School and Hook Parish Hall. Services were held at Chessington and at the Alexander recreation ground, a 'Grand Carnival Procession' was held

104 *Winthrop House and Surbiton Station in the 1960s.*

through the streets, a 'Tiara Ball' was held at the assembly rooms, and Bob Monkhouse presented a 'Midnight Matinee' at the Odeon.

The Surbiton Lagoon remained popular through this period; it was not closed until 1979. Attendances soared at Chessington Zoo, which welcomed over 4,500 people over the Easter Bank holiday in 1954. In 1956 a model village opened at the zoo and in 1963 a new bar and restaurant were added. Day trips were also organised by British Rail from Surbiton to seaside resorts such as Brighton, which could be reached for 7½d. The Ace of Spades remained popular for dining and dancing and opened a new grill room in July 1955, though this was gutted the following year. Dancing

was also held at the assembly rooms, where improvements costing £4,000 were made to the ballroom in 1961. The Navy League organised activity sessions at Raven's Ait, which received mains electricity in 1954. Canine fashions of the period were reflected in the opening of a 'Poodle Parlour' at Brighton Road in 1961.

April 1955 saw the 21st birthday of the Surbiton Odeon Cinema. Champagne was served and the Mayor, Mrs. Bidmead said; 'We are proud of this cinema in Surbiton'. But cinema visits tailed off locally in the following decade, and Tolworth Odeon was demolished in February 1961 to make way for the Tolworth tower. The Surbiton Odeon finally closed in 1975.

Surbiton retained, as always, its less respectable side. In the early 1960s, *Scanty's*, *Black Nylons* and *Exotica* magazines were printed and published in Surbiton by 'Glamour House' and 'Compete' of St Mark's Hill.

The End of Surbiton Borough

The population of Surrey increased by about nineteen thousand between 1946 and 1953. This meant that Surrey was entitled to be represented by one more MP; and Surbiton, along with two wards of Epsom and Ewell, was chosen to form Surrey's new electoral district.

The proposal was backed by Mr. Reynolds, leader of the Labour Group on Surbiton Council, who remarked: 'Surbiton is swamped by the old Tory atmosphere of the Royal Borough. The Labour Party is far better organised in Surbiton'. In the event, Nigel Fisher won the new seat for the Conservatives in the May 1955 General Election.

Having gained its own MP, Surbiton was faced with a new threat to its municipal independence. A Government White Paper proposed the formation of a local authority from Esher, Weybridge, Walton, Kingston, Malden and Surbiton, with the option of adding parts of northern Epsom. The new authority, as part of Greater London, would take over responsibility in areas previously controlled by the county council, including education.

105 *The diving board at Surbiton Lagoon, c.1960.*

Esher, Walton and Weybridge strongly opposed the plan from the beginning. Malden was also opposed, wishing to merge instead with Wimbledon, while Kingston remained lukewarm. But the proposals were officially supported by Surbiton's ruling Conservatives although several individual Conservative members remained strongly opposed. The proposals were also opposed by the Labour Group on the Council.

The issue was debated by the council at a special meeting on 12 March 1962. Councillor Reynolds of the Labour Group forecast a breakdown in local government if the plan was accepted while Conservative Councillor Granville-Smith envisaged the scheme providing 'diminished representation in return for greatly increased costs'. But Councillor Beresford spoke to allay fears that Surbiton would lose its sense of identity if the plan were carried forward. In his view, Surbiton would continue to exist 'through the spirit of organisations and societies within it'.

By 21 votes to 14, the proposals were accepted. In spite of this, Councillor Greenwood claimed that 95 per cent of Surbiton residents were opposed to the plan. Public discontent with the council was fuelled by a large rise in borough rates announced in February 1963. By then it appeared that the council had overspent. According to a spokesman, 'there was nothing left talking about' in the borough balances.

Esther and Weybridge won their fight to remain part of Surrey, but Malden was forced to unite with Surbiton in the new Royal Borough of Kingston. Alderman Cyril Judge of Kingston was elected as first mayor of the new borough on 13 January 1965, with Alderman Healey of Surbiton as his deputy. In his first speech as mayor, Alderman Judge stressed that all residents 'need be under no apprehension that local identities would be lost'.

He appealed to all members of the new combined council to unite in the service of the 146,000 people of the new borough. Alderman Edwards promised, in support of the proposals: 'Although Surbiton becomes part of Kingston it will always be known as the 'Queen of the Suburbs'.

Epilogue

Surbiton reached the national headlines in 1968 when workers at the Colt Factory in Surbiton launched the 'I'm Backing Britain' campaign. Chessington Zoo has maintained its national profile and is now the site of one of Britain's leading theme parks. Work began in 1978 on Surbiton YMCA and Sainsbury's as part of the Surbiton Central Area Plan.

The destruction of Surbiton's Victorian heritage has been slowed by the establishment of conservation areas and the listing of buildings. The Kingston Society fought to make Southborough a conservation area, while the Surbiton and District Historical Society works to increase awareness of local history. Many of Surbiton's most important buildings are now protected, including Regency Cottage and other buildings on Ewell Road, Southborough House, 124-126 Maple Road, South Terrace, St Andrew's Church and the shop front at 12 Victoria Road. Castle Hill, St Mary's Church and Vane Cottage have listed status in Chessington.

The 1995 division of the borough of Kingston into neighbourhoods, responsible for local concerns, has restored some degree of autonomy to areas which were formerly independent of Kingston. With spacious streets, relatively low crime, good schools and a depth of historical associations, Surbiton, Tolworth, Hook and Chessington remain privileged places to live and work as integral parts of Britain's 'Top Town'.

INDEX

Ace of Spades, 104, 124
Acre Hill, 73
Addison Avenue, 110
Adelaide Road, 29, 59, 69
Albury House, 31, 33, 102, 116
Alexandra recreation ground, 53, 95, 104, 111, 113, 114
Allen's Drapers, 85
Alpine Avenue, 1
Alpha Road, 18, 37, 45, 93, 115
allotments, 105
Alwin, 5
Ames, Councillor, 105
Anderson, 10
Andre Rubber Co. Ltd., 97, 118
Antrobus, Sir Edmund, 26
Argyle House, 49
Arlington Road, 44
Arundel, Lord, 10
Ashcombe Avenue, 18, 22, 113
Ashtead Villa, 1
assembly rooms, 22, 59, 60, 73, 83, 103, 123, 124
Audley, Major Lewis, 10, 13, 14
Aubrey, 10, 14, 15
Avenue, The, 49, 51, 53
Avenue Elmers, 51, 53, 60

Baggallay QC, 71
Balaclava Road, 44, 77
Baldwin, Stanley, 89
Banstead Downs, 10, 13
Barnado, Dr., 62
Barnes, Thomas, 44
Bartlett Ashmead, 29
Barwell Court, 1, 3, 10
Beaconsfield Road, 77
beggars, 64
Berg's builders, 96
Berkeley, Stanley, 62
Berowe, 4

Berrylands, 15, 18, 97; Estate, 29; Farm, 18, 77, 96; Lawn Tennis Club, 50; Road, 19, 96, 105; Station, 96
Berry Lodge Farm, 18
Bestall, Alfred, 104
Betty Joel Printers, 97
Bidder QC, 70, 71
Biden, 20
Bidemead, Councillor, 124
Blitz, 108-110
Blomfield, Sir Arthur, 41
Blyton, Enid, 104
Bolton Close, 114
Boxley Abbey, 8, 10
Braemore House, 50
Brassey, Thomas, 22
brickmaking, 15, 16, 24, 26, 29, 30, 71
Bridge, Alderman, 112
Brighton Road, 18, 23, 33, 38, 50, 53, 83, 86, 110
British Restaurants, 110, 111
Broad Lane, 17
Bronze Age, 1
Broomfield Road, 95
Brown, Robert, 38
Browne, Balfour, 71
Browns Road, 38, 51, 53
Bryant, Wilberforce, 52
Buckingham, Duke of, 10
Burdett-Coutts, Angela, 29, 40, 41
Burney, Rev. Charles, 39, 50, 65
Burney, Fanny, 16
Burnt Stub, 9, 104
buses, 79, 83
Butler, Charles, 101
Byhurst Farm, 103

Cadogan Road, 30, 53
Castle Hill, 1, 3, 8

Callenders Cable and Construction Co., 78, 80
Capability Brown, 16
Cave, Sir Ambrose, 7
Chapell, Edward, 25
Chesea Water Co., 31, 50, 53
Chessington; airport (proposed) 103; Church, 8, 9, 98; Church Fields recreation ground, 113; Common, 20, 22; Community Centre, 116; Court Estate, 98, 114; Dean of, 15; Development Company, 114; enclosure, 7, 20, 22; Hall Estate, 115; Manor at Hook (see also Fream) 7, 8, 10, 22; new housing, 97, 98, 112, 114, 115; origins of name, 7; South Station, 89; Zoo, 104, 110, 116, 117, 124
Chetwynd-Stapleton, Rev., 72
Christ Church, 39, 40
Christchurch National School, 45
Christchurch Primary, 116
civil defence, 105-109
Claremont Gardens, 101
Claremont; Hall, 18; House, 44, 53; Road, 29, 73, 83, 85, 120
Clarendon, 10, 14
Clark, Petula, 114
Claygate, 4
Clay Hill/Lane, 23, 53
Clayton Road, 93, 114
Cleaveland Road, 53
Clements, Robert, 26
Clerk, William, 30
Clocktower, 73, 78, 115
Coleman, M., 54
Coleman, Dr. Owen, 54, 73, 83
Colt Heating and Ventilating, 97, 126
Copt Gilders, 98
Comte de Paris, 44
Congregational Church, 44, 49, 50

Connolly, Maureen, 50
Cooper, Sir Alfred, 53, 73, 75
Colcock, Theophilus, 9
Coronation Cinema, 83
Coronation festivities, 104, 123, 124
Corbett and McClymont, 40, 51
Corkran, Charles, 18, 35, 36, 38,
    52
Corkran Road, 115
Cottage Grove, 25
Cottenham, Lord, 23
Coulthurst, William, 43, 51
Coutts, 26-9, 35
Cowley, William, 43, 51
Cox Lane, 20, 113, 117
Cranborne Avenue, 114, 117
Cranes Estate, 51
Crawter, Thomas, 19, 20
Cripps QC, 71
Crisp, Samuel, 16
Cromwell, Oliver, 9
Croylands, 110
Cundy, Captain, 52
Curling, Mr., 18, 38, 43
Cutmore, Councillor, 116

Dalbier, Major, 10
Decoy, The, 10, 13, 14
le Despenser, Hugh, 5
Devonshire House, 115
Dewhurst, Jane, 61, 62
Dixey, Phyllis, 104
Dorking, 13
Douglas Road, 110
Drummonds, 26-8
Duke of Chartres, 44
Duke of Monpensier, 44
Duke and Duchess of Teck, 59
Dunnage, Mr., 31
Dunnage, Laura, 75
Durnford, William, 35
Dyson Coal and Coke Merchants,
    84

Ede, Chuter, 99
Edmer, 7
Edmund, Duke of Kent, 5
Edmund, Duke of Cornwall, 8
Edward I, 8
Edward III, 4
Edward VII, 62, 73, 78
Edward VIII, 100
Edwards, Alderman, 115, 126
Egmont Garden City, 95
Egmont, Lord, 71, 72

electricity supply of, 70, 78, 79
Electric Parade, 86
Electric Southern Railway, 89
Elizabeth, 10, 35
Ellingham School, 116
Elmes, James, 26
Elmers, 16, 35
Elmers Estate, 51
Emperor of Brazil, 44
Enclosure, 19
Epsom Rural District, 97, 98
Esher, 68
evacuation, 113
Evelyn, John, 7
Ewell Road, 19, 24, 30, 38, 44, 67,
    70, 73, 83, 86, 93, 97, 111

Farmers, W.B., (Butchers), 81
Fassett, Thomas, 16
Fire Brigade, 54
Fisher, Nigel, 124
Fishponds, 9, 16, 101, 105
Forster, E.M., 61
Fox and Nicholls, 97
Fream Manor, 7, 10, 15, 22
Friar, Thomas, 10
Frierson, Henry, 10, 14
Fullers Way estate, 115
fundraising, 110-12

Gables Theatre, 52, 73, 74, 75
Gala Factory, 117, 118
Galley, Richard, 19
Gampell, Mrs. Sydney, 112
Garratt, John, 17
Garrick, 16
Garrison Lane, 7, 8, 16, 114
General Strike, 89
Gibbon, Major, 13
Giles, Mr., 22
Glenbuck Road, 53
Goddard, Richard, 104
Gordon, Robert, 71
Gosbury Hill, 114, 116, 123
Goss, Henry, 20
Gosse, Joseph, 16
Grand Avenue, 96, 105
Grapelleingeham, 2
Green Belt, 114, 115
Griffin Hotel, 44

Hall, Sir Benjamin, 35
Hamilton, Christopher, 15, 16
Hardwicke, Philip, 39
Hardy, Thomas, 61

Harley Motors, 112
Harrow on the Hill, 14
Hatton, Thomas, 10, 16
Haycroft Estate, 96
Healey, Alderman, 115, 126
Helena Rubenstein Factory, 97
Henderson, Sir Neville, 110
Henry III, 8
Hill House, 17
Hillcroft College, 52, 102, 103, 105
hockey club, 50
Hook, 2, 4, 18; Air Force Base, 105;
    Bowls Club, 91; Community
    Centre, 116; drainage, 55;
    National School, 48; Parish Hall,
    111; recreation ground, 77;
    underpass, 122
Hog, John, 2
Hoggart, Edward, 27
Hook Rise, 96, 117
Hook Road, 104
Hoke, Thomas, 9
Holland, Earl of, 10, 11, 13, 14
Hollyfield Road, 95
Hollyfield School, 32, 116
Horticultural Society, 50
Howard Road, 93
Howell, Bulmer, 68
hunting, 32
Hussie, Cecily, 9

Ice Age, 1
Imworth, 19
incendiary raids, 112
Indian cricket club, 50
inns; Anchor, 52; Black Lion, 33, 86;
    Bonesgate Inn, 66, King's Head, 27;
    Railway Tavern, 23, 32, Red Lion;
    20, 79; Spread Eagle, 52; Waggon
    and Horses, 15, 17, 35
Isold, Hugh of, 7
Ivimey, Joseph, 59

Jeffries, Richard, 61, 71
Jellicoe, Admiral, 63
Jemmett, Charles, 20, 36
Jemmett, family, 51
Jemmett, Rev. John, 77
Johnson, Dr., 16
Joint Sewage Board, 86
Judge, Cyril, Alderman, 126

Kavanagh, Stephen, 71, 83, 86
Kew Palace, 20
King Charles I, 10

King Charles Bridge, 58
King Charles Road, 14, 18, 38
Kingston; almshouses, 23; bailiffs, 9, 19; Batalion Surrey National Reserve, 87; boundaries, 34-5; by-pass, 89, 95, 96, 117, 122, 123; commons, 9, 13, 15, 19, 22; Corporation, 18, 23, 26, 31, 33, 34, 53; Endowed Charities, 51; Extension Bill, 64-71; Gas Company, 80; Grammar School, 9, 71; Highway Board, 83; Hundred, 1; Improvement Acts, 34; Royal Manor of, 2, 5; Rural Sanitary Authority, 55, 72
Kingston Society, 126
Kitchener, Lord, 87

Labour Party, 112, 125
Lailey, Nicholson, 86
Lamberts Road, 53
Lambeth Waterworks, 31
Lane, J. and Son, 82
Langley Avenue, 55, 97
Langley Sarah and Thomas, 18
Lapidge, 16
Largewood Avenue, 110
Lavers, Mr., 41
Leach, Alderman, 114
Leavers, W., 44
lighting, 35, 37
lime kiln, 18
Lingfield Avenue, 78, 95
Livesey, Sir Miles, 13
Long Ditton, 68
Lovelace, Earl of, 53, 72, 77
Lovelace Estate, 10
Lower Marsh Lane, 23, 93
LSWR, 22, 57
Lumley, Lord, 10

Maori Sports Ground, 110
Majorbanks, Edward, 26, 51
Malden and Coombe, 64
Malden Rushett, 72, 103
Mansfield Road, 103, 105
Maple Road, 18, 37, 40, 50, 78, 115
de Merton, Walter, 8
McNutt, Canon, 87
Mear, Councillor, 108
Melcombe House, 49
Melton, Harriet, 29
Merryweather, 22, 26
Merton College, 8, 10, 16

Merton Priory, 2, 4, 5, 7, 10
Middle Green Lane, 18, 37
Middle Stone Age, 1
Moderate, The, 10
Mollart Engineering, 97, 112
Monkhouse, Bob, 124
Moody, Helen Wills, 50
Moor Lane School, 98, 116, 123

Nash, 18, 22
Native Guano Company, 55
Neale, William, 19
New Kingston, 25-6
New Stone Age, 1
NHS offices, 116
Nonsuch Park, 7, 10, 13
North Tolworth Manor, 5, 7
Northcote Avenue, 114
Nottage Henry, 25
Nuthall, Betty, 94

Oak Hill Lodge, 52
Oakcroft Estate, 96
Oaklands Chapel, 44
Odeon Cinemas, 104, 110, 114, 124
Omnibus Bill, 77
Opticrafts, 97
Our Lady Immaculate Church, 117

Palace Road, 115
Parish pound, 16
Parker, Charles, 30
Parnall Aircraft, 97
Paton, Dr., 73
Penney, William, 20
Perrers, Alice, 4
Phillips, Rev. Edward, 35, 40
Pigache, George, 64
Pine Gardens, 116
de Planaz, Ralph, 5
Polhill, Nathaniel, 71
police station, 53
Pooley, Alexander, 24, 25, 27
Pooley, Thomas, 24-9
Portsmouth Road, 62, 64, 69, 83, 113
Poulter, Mrs., 33
Pressly, Charles, 30
Primitive Methodist Chapel, 44
Prince of Wales, 41, 53
Princess of Wales, 73, 75
Prince Leopold, 44
Princess Charlotte, 44
Princess Frederica, 49
Princess Louise Marie Therese, 44

Pritty, Colonel, 13
private schools, 49, 50
prostitution, problem of, 64

Queen's Promenade, 53
Queen Victoria, 53, 56, 73

Railway; Bill, 1835, 22; cutting, 21; extension to Chessington, 89; extension to Guildford, 57; route of, 22, 23; see also Surbiton, Chessington South Stations

Raeburn Avenue, 101, 105
Ransom & Luck, 114
Raphael, Alexander, 30
Rastrick, Mr., 53
rates, 53, 77
Ratledge, W.A., 84
Raven's Ait, 1, 24, 46, 50
Ravenscar Road, 110
Red Lion Road/Lane, 86, 93, 95
Redhill, 13
regatta, 46
Reigate, 13
Retreat, The, 53
Reynolds, Councillor, 114, 125
Rich, Henry, 11, 13, 14
Richardson, Rowley, 28, 29, 31, 34, 35, 37, 39, 51, 55
Richmond, Duke of, 10
roads, condition of, 13, see also turnpikes
Roffee, William, 16
Rowe, Eliza, 61
Royal Army Medical Corp, 87
Ruxley Lane, 114
Rychbell, John, 10

St Andrew's Church, 40, 41, 103
St Andrew's Square, 51, 93, 105
St George's Church, 103, 117
St James' Road, 59, 60
St Leonard's Road, 30, 38, 62
St Mark's Church, 29, 31, 32, 38, 39, 88, 103, 110; St Mark's Hill, 29, 83, 125
St Mark's School, 35, 38, 45
St Matthew's Church, 41, 43, 95, 105
St Matthew's School, 49
St Paul's Church, Hook, 18, 39, 44
St Paul's School, Hook, 48, 95
St Raphael Chapel, 30, 44
'Salute the Soldier', 111

Sainsbury's, 126
Sales, Thomas, 20
sanitation, 31, 38, 55, 86
Sanger, W., 100
Scott, Sir Claude, 26
Seething Wells, 15, 31, 33, 37
Seifert, Richard, 117
Selfe, John, 24, 26, 29, 30
servants, 32, 33
Shrublands Estate, 24, 29
Siebe, Gorman, 117
Silver Jubilee, 104
Simpson, J., 38
Skerne, William, 4
Solartron, 117
South Bank, 52, 53, 78
South Bank Terrace, 24, 30
South Tolworth Manor, 5, 7
Southampton Hotel, The, 32, 35, 117
Southborough Estate, 22, 52, 126
Southborough Hill, 24
Southborough Lodge, 18, 35
sports, 50
Stane Street, 1
Stevens, John, 26, 28, 29
Sterry, Mrs., 50
Stickley, family, 65, 66, 67
Strange, Thomas, 18, 19, 24
strike, 32, 33, 86
Surbiton; Beagles, 73; Borough Charter, 98-100, Borough coat of arms, 100; Borough Charter celebrations, 104; Borough Council, proceedings of, 103, 104; Borough, end of, 125, 126; Common, 9, 13, 15, 16, 18, 19, 22; Cricket Club, 50; death rate, 54; Drying and Cleaning Works, 81; Golf Glub, 50; Grammar School, 102, 116; High School, 102; Hill, 17, 18, 20, 22, 23, 38, 54; Hill Estate, 29, 30, 96; Hill House, 20; Hill Road, 78; Hill Working Men's Club, 73; Hospital, 54, 101, 104, 108, 113, 116; Improvement Act, 35, 36; Improvement Commissioners, 36, 37, 38, 53, 64; Lagoon, 101, 110, 124, 125; library, 102, 116;

Odeon, 104, 110, 114, 124; origin of name, 2; Place, 17, 18, 36, 83; rates rise in, 53, 77; Reading Room, 50; redevelopment of, 115, 116; Station, 21, 23, 56, 57, 83, 89; social change, 75; Tonic sol-fa Club, 50; Tradesmen's Protection Society, 32; Urban District Authority, 64; Working Men's Club, 50; Young Men's Improvement Association, 50
Surbiton and District Historical Society, 126
Surrey County Council Order, 1933, 97, 98
Surrey Territorial Army, 87
Swarthy, Magnus, 8

Tatham, Thomas, 20
Terry, Christopher, 15, 18, 24
Terry's Lane, 18
Thackeray, 61
Thames Ditton, 68
Thames Sailing Club, 50
Thomas, Edward, 72
Thorne & Co., 95
Thorogoods, 95
Thick, Thomas, 26
Thirlway, E., 115
Tiffin School, 71
Times, The, 26
Tolworth; Broadway, 110, 121; enclosure of, 6, 20; Congregational Church, 103; Co-op Hall, 111; dairy farm, 93; development of, 97; drainage of, 55; origin of name, 5; Court Manor and Farm, 5, 6, 7, 15, 71, 83, 86, 93; fountain, 80, 86; Girls' School, 102; Hospital, 72; merger with Surbiton, 71; North Tolworth Manor, 5, 7; Odeon, 104, 114, 117, 119, 124; Park Road, 113; Pond, 83, 86; South Tolworth Manor, 5, 7; Tostig Earl, 4; tower, 117, 119, 124
tramways, 79, 83
trolley buses, 123
turnpike roads, 15, 16, 17, 53

United Temperance Association, 54
Uxbridge, Earl of, 16
Uxbridge Road, 30, 69, 113, 115

V1s, 112
VE celebrations, 114
Victoria Avenue, 111
Victoria Road, 29, 53, 122
Villiers Close, 110
Villiers, Lord Francis, 10, 12, 14
Villiers Road, 14

Wadbrook, George, 16
Wadbrook, Harriet, 24
Wadbrook, William, 24, 26, 27
Walpole, Charles, 35, 36
Walter, William, 20, 29, 30, 36, 38, 101
Walton, Sir William, 36
'War Weapons Week', 110
Warren Drive, 99, 105
Watercress and flower girls, 76
Wateville, Robert de, 8
Wentworth Court, 93
Wesleyan Chapel, 44
Wesleyan Church, 44, 45
Westergate House, 69
Western Electric, 97
Westfield Road, 30, 38
Wigod of Wallingford, 8
windmill, 18, 24
White Cross Prison, 27
White House, 17, 19, 24
White, Percy, 61
Whitehall Crescent, 113
Williams, Dr., 102
Wimbledon Championship, 50, 94
Wimpey, 96
Winthrop House, 117
Woodbines, 15
Woodgate Amy, 89, 108
Woods, William, 30
Woodward's *Miscellany*, 15
workhouse, 15
WVS, 108, 113

YMCA, 126

Zimmern, family, 62, 77